Larry,
..Here you go ~ I real
live autographed copy ~
Thanks for asking ~

RELATIONSHIPS *from* **ADDICTION** *to* AUTHENTICITY

RELATIONSHIPS

from **ADDICTION** *to*

AUTHENTICITY

Claudine Pletcher and Sally Bartolameolli, M.Ed.

Health Communications, Inc.
Deerfield Beach, Florida

www.hcibooks.com

Library of Congress Cataloging-in-Publication Data
is available through the Library of Congress.

ISBN-10: 0-7573-0746-9
ISBN-13: 978-0-7573-0746-1

Publisher: Health Communications, Inc.
        3201 S.W. 15th Street
        Deerfield Beach, FL 33442-8190

Cover photo ©Claudine Pletcher
Cover design by Larissa Hise Henoch
Interior design and formatting by Lawna Patterson Oldfield

Contents

Foreword

by John Bradshaw

There is a relatively unknown but devastating emotional disorder that affects women of all ages and cultures. It has been potentially present since the first pair of humans flirted, romanced each other, and had sexual intercourse. Over the centuries, with the slow demise of patriarchal dominance (which is by no means gone), the nature of this disorder—called *co-sex addiction**—has become increasingly known and understood. [*Authors' note*: terms that are italicized and followed by an asterisk appear with full definitions in the glossary at the back of the book.] Probably an inestimable number of women have gone to their deaths carrying an unspoken sense of shame-flawed identity—as well as their repressed anger and desolate feelings of loneliness because they were unaware that they were co-sex addict victims.

Pletcher and Bartolameolli make it clear that the core of the co-sex disorder is toxic or *carried shame.** *Shame** is one of the nine innate emotions. Shame safeguards our spirituality as it lets us know our limits, especially when related to pleasure, interest, and sexuality. Innate shame is a natural boundary. When we are violated by an overpowering person, our boundaries are damaged. When an abusive sex addict violates a co-sex addict victim, the co-sex addict carries the addict's shame as a sickness of the soul, whose major symptom is silence.

Co-sex addiction as a disease has been kept silent because it is rooted in the toxic shamelessness of sex addicts. As victims, co-sex addicts feel powerless to speak out and set appropriate boundaries.

Claudine Pletcher, whom I have known for forty years, and Sally Bartolameolli have vividly and dramatically given voice to the disease of co-sex addiction. Each experience is firsthand. I have personally witnessed Claudine's journey—step-by-step—from beginning to end. I have marveled at her courage and tenacity. I see this book as her desire for justice and as a need for both authors to expose this awful disorder.

Pletcher and Bartolameolli are undisputed experts on the subject of co-sex addiction. They know more about it than anyone I know and have presented an exposé that with great clarity supersedes anything I have read before. Their work has clarified many aspects of co-sex addiction of which I was not fully aware. For example, there are many therapists who confuse co-sex addiction with love and/or *sex addiction*.* While there are similar elements in all addictions, distinguishing between the unique differences that allow us to call one addiction by a special name is a critical factor in the *recovery** from that addiction.

What Pletcher and Bartolameolli make extraordinarily clear is that what makes co-sex addiction so difficult to recover from is that it is also rooted in the dysfunctional *enculturation** of women. This includes the "normal" abusive dysfunction that society accepts as women's roles. The most severe forms of co-sex addict behavior are rooted in early abuse, neglect, or *enmeshment** in their parents' marital dysfunction or individual neediness.

Co-sex addiction, as a result of generations of male dominance that has persisted since the beginning of patriarchy, includes the acceptance and normalization of the inequality and submission of women. It has taken generations to really see the morbidity and heinousness of what has been considered a woman's normal role in family life and normal male sexual dominance in male/female relationships. Co-sex addiction certainly exists among gays and lesbians, but it is primarily a disorder that affects the lives of women who are in a "traditional" male/female relationship.

Pletcher and Bartolameolli have lived through the dismal agony of shame, silence, and the loneliness that characterizes co-sex addiction, and they have carefully dissected both its cause and how it reaches its critical apex. Especially powerful is their analysis of the offender/victim polarity. This shows how the sex addict operates as the *Big Offender** and softens his offensive behavior by being the *little victim** (the one raged at and criticized by his exasperated spouse). The co-sex addict who is the *Big Victim** can become a *little offender** by either emotionally or physically abusing her children or perhaps by developing other relationships outside the primary relationship, sexually or otherwise. Co-sex addicts' greatest sleight of hand is the dynamic of using their less-offensive victimization of others to create mood-altering *guilt** and shame over their *little offender* behavior.

In our present culture, with sexual shamelessness at an all-time high, I cannot imagine a more important book than this one. Sex addicts, of whatever kind, simply cannot continue their addiction if there are no unrecovering co-sex addicts to be their victims. This includes women who pose for pornography, act in sex films, and appear on the Internet; phone sex workers; massage parlor matrons; prostitutes; and the "normal-looking" wife who is the object of her sex-addicted, "normal-looking" husband. As the stories in the book dramatically illustrate, many women have had enough—and as the disease of co-sex addiction is fully understood (and this book goes a long way in helping us understand it), the loving intimacy and sacredness of sexuality that constitutes the physical love between the sexes has a chance of being restored.

In his book, *The Soul of Sex*, Thomas Moore speaks of the age-old mythologies where the phallic and vaginal mysteries were understood and celebrated as sacred. If ever a culture needed spiritual recovery and the blessings of awe, mystery, and sacredness of sexuality, it is our own.

I consider it an absolute honor to be asked by Claudine Pletcher and Sally Bartolameolli to write a foreword to their book. I do so with full awareness of my own covert chauvinism and recovering sexual addiction. I've learned a lot by reading this book. I fancy that there is a great deal in this book that is urgent for the enhancing of our understanding of rich, *authentic intimacy** and sexuality, as well as truly healthy families.

Preface

Our purpose in writing this book and our desire for everyone who reads it is that they be empowered to create in their lives "authentic relationships." The journey of writing this book has been a significant part of our journey in recovery. We offer our combined experience of almost forty-five years in 12-step spiritual recovery. In the process of writing and publishing this book, we very humbly believe we are living the 12 steps of our Co-Sex Addicts Anonymous program.

While the journey of recovery follows a detailed and structured 12-step process, we also have a much deeper and more universal intention in writing this book: we believe there is no time our society has been more ready and eager to receive this message. It is our desire that a Sacred Feminine Voice be restored to its proper place in our culture. Addressing the ever-powerful disease of co-sex and sex addiction is an essential beginning.

In our co-sex addiction recovery, we honor the feminine voice, which very loudly declares that we will no longer carry nor *enable** the shame of our offenders. We are no longer victims in our own lives. We learn this by first learning to love and respect ourselves. This means that, as women, we learn to set boundaries, honor our inner intuition and knowledge, and demand to be heard, appreciated, and treated with the respect we deserve. Then we teach this to those we are in relationship with, model this new behavior for our children, and share this knowledge with the women and men in our lives.

Sexuality is also deeply impacted on this journey of recovery. We learn to experience *authentic intimacy*,* and this translates to sexual intimacy. For perhaps the first time in our lives, we are fully awakened and present to the sexual experience. We are moved deeply, and in many ways, this new way of relating becomes a spiritual experience as well.

Eventually, this deep respect and honor we develop for ourselves on our journey transfers globally. We are available now to listen within for our own purpose and calling of service and contribution. We are ready to do as we are directed in the twelfth step of our spiritual recovery program, which is to "carry this message to others and practice these principles in all areas of our lives."

Disclaimer: The stories and examples in this book are about co-sex addiction. We are grateful to all the women who shared their stories with us and gave us permission to share parts or all of their stories with you. You may relate to and recognize some of what is shared as part of your own experience. This commonality reflects the elements of the co-sex addiction disease. Details have been changed and altered to honor confidentiality and anonymity. The stories are shared and given with permission to print for the service and healing of other women who still suffer.

We refer to a "Higher Power" throughout the book. We use various terms that are interchangeable to describe this "Higher Power" (God, Spiritual Source, etc.) with the intention of respecting the diverse spiritual practices of all individuals.

The examples in this book illustrate the dynamics that occur between a co-sex addict and sex addict generally portrayed in a female/male relationship. It is our experience and opinion that this dynamic occurs within gay and lesbian partnerships as well.

Often when reading books of this nature, we find that it will *push our buttons*. This means that we may feel agitated or irritated by what we read. When this happens, it is a good time to stop and reflect on the issues that are mirroring to us our own pain that originated in our *family of origin** and to become aware of the work yet to be done. This may be an opportunity for your greatest healing. Remember, this is a normal reaction when old wounds and painful memories are reintroduced to you and stirring to be released and healed.

We encourage you to have 12-step support groups to attend, counseling and therapists familiar with co-sex and sex addiction, and trustworthy allies to reach out to regularly. We believe this support you create will lead you to a deeper spiritual connection, and we welcome you to the adventure of recovery.

1

What Is
Co-Sex Addiction?

*A*ddiction,* according to *The Consolidated Webster Encyclopedia Dictionary*, is defined as "the act of devoting or giving up of one's self to a practice." The sex addict is addicted to sex for a *fix*,* and the co-sex addict is addicted to the sex addict and the relationship. A co-sex addict may not only give her body, but may also give her time, emotional energy, financial resources, creativity, or her very soul over to her sex addict to fill the emptiness inside.

In our culture, we often hear about alcohol, drug addiction, eating disorders, workaholics, violence, gambling problems, and a host of other compulsive-addictive behaviors. The prevalence of sex addiction has now captured our attention. Computer pornography, rape, incest, molestation by religious officials, exhibitionism, prostitution, child pornography, and multiple affairs are all examples of sex addiction. The use of sex to avoid being responsible for one's own needs or feelings, or to medicate or cover up one's feelings of any sort, involves sex and co-sex addiction. The sex addict may use one or any variety of these various sources for his fix. This may or may not include using the relationship for sex in order to fix his feelings.

With each occurrence of sexual *acting out** and sex addiction, there is the presence of co-sex addiction. Co-sex addicts are the individuals who are willing, either consciously or unconsciously, to give themselves over to another's addiction and be used to provide the fix. This is a co-sex addict's way to attempt to fill her internal emptiness by "hoping" to solidify, create, or mend a relationship. This is how she gets *her* fix.

When addiction and the *addictive cycle** is present in one's life, getting a fix from the addiction or addict becomes the center of one's life and energy. (Both individuals "give up themselves," as the *Webster* dictionary defined addiction, to practice their sex addiction and co-sex addiction.) It fills the space of what could be an authentic/healthy relationship with an obsessive-compulsive drive to fill the cravings and get that fix. Addictive behavior repels intimacy and an authentic relationship.

BEGINNING CO-SEX ADDICTION RECOVERY

Most women come into healing and recovery from co-sex addiction because of the discovery of their partner's sex addiction and actions pertaining to it. Sometimes it is about someone else's addiction close to them, such as a brother, father, or friend. Initially, we think that the trouble is the other person or the relationship itself. However, what one learns over time during recovery from co-sex addiction is that the source of the dysfunction is not in the relationship with others, but in the relationship with oneself. Before one can have an authentic relationship with another, one must have an authentic relationship with oneself.

Authentic relationship with oneself is about knowing our herstory/history (*family of origin work**). Once we know this, we grieve the loss of what we often thought was a happy childhood. We embrace the reality of how we were hurt and *set up** to be addicts/co-addicts with dysfunctional relationships. This is why we must look at any addiction that is in our lives. We will find that the co-sex/sex addiction we live with today was set up through our parents, extended family, or primary caregivers in our family of origin. This brings us into reality and eventually forgiveness of ourselves and our *abusers/offenders*.* Our family tree will be imprinted with the gifts of our recovery, and this will give birth to a profound spiritual healing for generations previous to us and generations to come.

In co-sex addiction recovery, we begin to develop tools to distinguish when our past hurts get *triggered*.* This tells us what old herstory/trauma is and what our present reality is. Recovery also provides a step-by-step process to assist in distinguishing *automatic behaviors*.* These old behaviors from the past lose their power, and we are free to choose behaviors based on our values today.

BEHAVIOR OF SEX ADDICTS AND CO-SEX ADDICTS

The following chart is a visual depiction of the behaviors exhibited by sex addicts and the corresponding behavior for co-sex addicts. Please keep in mind that some or all of the behavior may apply in any combination and/or at any given time. This addictive "dance" includes the behavior of each type of addict and how they most often fit together with a corresponding "step."

BEHAVIOR	SEX ADDICT	CO-SEX ADDICT
Affairs	Goes outside primary relationship for sex. Justification: I work hard, and I deserve some relaxation and pleasure.	Denies the affairs. Justification: Most men are unfaithful at least once.
Using prostitution	Goes outside primary relationship for contact or fix. Justification: She's cold. She never wants to have sex. No one will find out. I'll only do it once.	Denies or makes it about self. Tries to be more sexy, sleuths, checks pockets, credit cards, follows him. Justification: If only I were sexier, prettier, less demanding, wanted sex more, etc.

BEHAVIOR	SEX ADDICT	CO-SEX ADDICT
Compulsive masturbation	Using compulsive masturbation for a fix. Justification: I am not hurting anyone or endangering myself or my partnership with STDs.	Denies and/or ignores he is in the bathroom for long periods of time. Justification: He works hard and needs to relieve some pressure. (This may also get her off the hook for being used sexually.)
Pedophilia	Uses children sexually. Justification: Children are resilient, and they won't remember.	Denies. Justification: Blames the child. Blames self for not meeting his sexual needs.
Pornography, computer, and/or phone sex	Uses technology for sex fix. Justification: I am not hurting anyone and/or I need some relief.	Denies, tolerates, and may participate outside of own value system and wants. Justification: At least he is not hurting anyone else.
Exhibitionism /voyeurism	Exposes self and/or has compulsive/obsessive focus on sexual activities or objects. (This can be as subtle as going without proper clothes in the house.) Justification: I am not having intercourse, molesting anyone, etc.	Denies and/or blames self and tolerates inappropriate behavior outside of value system. Justification: All men are overfocused on sex; at least he is not hurting anyone. What goes on inside our own home is only our business.

BEHAVIOR	SEX ADDICT	CO-SEX ADDICT
Demanding sex from partner	Pressuring, raping, and/or forcing someone to have sex without full consent.	Tolerates this inappropriate behavior, feigns illness, causes conflict before bedtime, convinces herself it is her place to have sex even if she does not want to do so, etc.
	Justification: She is my wife, partner, girlfriend and/or at least I am not unfaithful.	Justification: At least he is not unfaithful, he wants me, etc. Also believes this will "secure" and "cement" the relationship.
Uses partner to have sex to avoid dealing with feelings	Uses someone else for sex.	Takes responsibility for fixing her partner's feelings with sex and absorbs those feelings so that both can have the temporary fix and illusion of power and control.
	Justification: She is my wife, partner, girlfriend, etc. I am a highly sexual person and/or I deserve to feel good.	Justification: If I give him sex, maybe he will leave me alone. He works hard, really wants me, etc. (continually confuses sex with love).
Male *sexual anorexia**	Is void of sexual desire or feelings.	Tolerates this lack of sexual contact, often for many years. Uses this as an excuse not to deal with the issues in the relationship.
	Justification: I'm just not a sexual person, I work hard, I'm tired, etc.	Justification: He just needs me to be patient, and at least he is not acting out. Maybe if I look better or sexier, am less demanding, etc., he will want me.

Co-sex and sex addiction can be acted out within committed relationships where no outside sexual activity takes place. One or both partners use sex to medicate/avoid feelings or try to cement or secure the relationship. Oftentimes this dynamic may be subtle, unconscious, or both.

Example: For years the wife of a surgeon would be sure to give her doctor husband sex the night before he went into surgery. In this exchange, the wife would actually "fix" or "medicate" her husband's fear, and he would then go "fearlessly" into the operating room. Sex was the vehicle for the sex addict to avoid being responsible for dealing directly with his fears, concerns, and feelings of inadequacy. Sex was the vehicle for the co-sex addict to avoid being responsible for dealing directly with her own fear, sense of over-responsibility, powerlessness, and human feelings of inadequacy as well. He gets a fix from the sex. She gets a fix from the illusion of "fixing" the addict with sex. The addictive cycle is now in place. The high from this addictive exchange is temporary. As it begins to diminish, the emptiness emerges and the need to get a fix from sex returns, as does the need to get a fix from fixing the addict.

Part of this dynamic is that the sex addict gets his feelings fixed with the sex and transfers feelings to the co-sex addict. The co-sex addict without recovery and boundaries then carries these feelings for her addict.

A MORE IN-DEPTH LOOK AT THE INTERNAL SYMPTOMS AND BEHAVIORS OF CO-SEX ADDICTION

While there is a particular "dance" that goes on between the sex addict and the co-sex addict, we also know there are many internalized beliefs and behaviors that characterize an unrecovering co-sex addict. Some or all of these may appear at any given time. These internalized beliefs and behaviors may also surface in some relationships and not others. Or they may simply be carried within our own thinking and evaluation of ourselves. The following is a list of beliefs and behaviors of a co-sex addict.

- Basing our feelings of value/worth on others' opinions of us.

- Tolerating verbal, physical, sexual, emotional, or financial abuse from anyone.

- Choosing clothing to provoke sexual attention or dressing very sloppily to deflect sexual attention.

- Getting a high from dressing provocatively or shutting down completely concerning appearance.

- Believing that our value as women is primarily connected to our physical/sexual appearance.

- Thinking there is not enough. We call this a *lack mentality**:
  we are not enough; we cannot generate enough income for ourselves; there are not enough men; there is not enough time; we are not pretty enough, smart enough, and so on.

- Being drawn to dysfunctional people and/or situations of high drama, chaos, and high intensity that are generated by people who are deceptive and/or abusive in some way.

- Constantly comparing ourselves to others, judging ourselves and/or others.

- Feeling superior or inferior to others (grandiosity, lack mentality/shame).

- Feeling afraid and threatened by others, particularly the "competition" (other women).

- Feeling that the world is full of enemies and/or the world is unfair.

- Isolating self from others, avoiding contact with others, and/or a fear of intimacy.

- Feeling victimized, being easily taken advantage of by others.

- Fear of being sexual and fear of own or others' sexuality.

- Being sexual with others to please them or gain their approval.

- Being sexual in ways outside of one's value system. Doing things sexually that are uncomfortable, degrading, scary, and/or unsafe.

- Not being able to say no when appropriate or to say yes when we really want to say yes.

- Fantasizing about relationships, being rescued or rescuing someone else, and so on.

- Confusing sex with love and love with sex.

- Using sexuality to punish or reward ourselves and/or others.

- Risking physical/emotional safety for a relationship. For example, putting oneself at risk for sexually transmitted disease.

- Neglecting our own hobbies, interests, dreams, and social circles to overfocus on the relationship and/or sex addict in our life.

- To "Velcro" the interests, dreams, and social circles of our partner.

- Using other substances to numb the pain (alcohol, food, nicotine, shopping, TV, etc.).

- Over-volunteering, excessive projects, commitments, and so on to avoid dealing with loss and pain in one's own life.

SYMPTOMS/BEHAVIORS OF
CO-SEX ADDICTION AND DISEASE IN RELATIONSHIPS

Sometimes it may be difficult to recognize our disorder and disease outside of our relationships with others. In addition to the "dance" of the sex addict and co-sex addict described earlier, we have identified some other patterns and behaviors that often occur within the relationship. These are dynamics that don't necessarily seem sexually oriented but that also occur within the addictive dynamic of a co-sex and sex-addicted relationship.

These behaviors may occur in isolation or in any combination. Some of the behaviors may occur within or outside of our primary romantic partnership.

- Partners have a pattern of raging, threatening to leave, and then staying over and over again.

- Relationship is characterized by a strong, persistent anxiety about the partner and the relationship.

- The co-sex addict consistently denies intuition and/or *innate sense** that something is wrong.

- Relationship is characterized by a constant feeling of being threatened in situations where other people are present.

- The co-sex addict frequently checks for signs that the partner is acting out by snooping, spying, checking pockets, reviewing Internet activity, and so on.

- The co-sex addict believes that she can control the addiction by throwing away her partner's pornography, changing her own behavior, changing her appearance, catering to sexual demands, and so on.

- There is a constant drive for attention/validation outside of relationships, sometimes in a sexual manner and sometimes in an emotional connection with another, through having an *emotional affair*.*

- A co-sex addict may become obsessively busy, involved with activities such as volunteering, workaholism, church, and so on.

- A co-sex addict may blame herself for her partner's addiction and blame her partner for her unhappiness/addiction.

- Either addict may create chaos, crisis, and drama to distract from the pain/addiction in the relationship.

- A co-sex addict may use sex to smooth over arguments, "fix" troubles, and make the addict feel better.

- There may be a drive to protect the addict and/or cover up the addict's behavior to family, friends, and society.

- There is a consistent rationalizing and minimizing of the addict's or her own addictive behavior, including her overeating, shopping, obsessing, bingeing and purging, and so on.

- In relationships, a co-sex addict may withhold sex as a threat and manipulation.

- A co-sex addict may provide sex to manipulate and/or gain a desired result, such as a vacation, new car, money, and so on.

- When a co-sex addict attempts to confront the behavior of her partner, there is a consistent pattern of the "reality being switched" (see *reality switch** in glossary), and she leaves the interaction with the *denial** of her reality about the addiction and takes on the reality of the sex addict.

ANOTHER VISUAL OF THE
CO-SEX AND SEX ADDICTION CYCLE

The next chart is a visual representation of the cycle of the co-sex addict with the "dance" of the sex addict. As is common in most addictive cycles, it begins with the desire for a "hit," followed by the fleeting "high" and feeling of "fulfillment." Next, the high wears off and the sinking feeling of emptiness returns, along with feelings of guilt and shame. Lastly, the co-sex addict seeks another hit and fix to abate the internal emptiness and pain, and then the cycle begins again.

Figure 1. Co-Sex Addictive Cycle

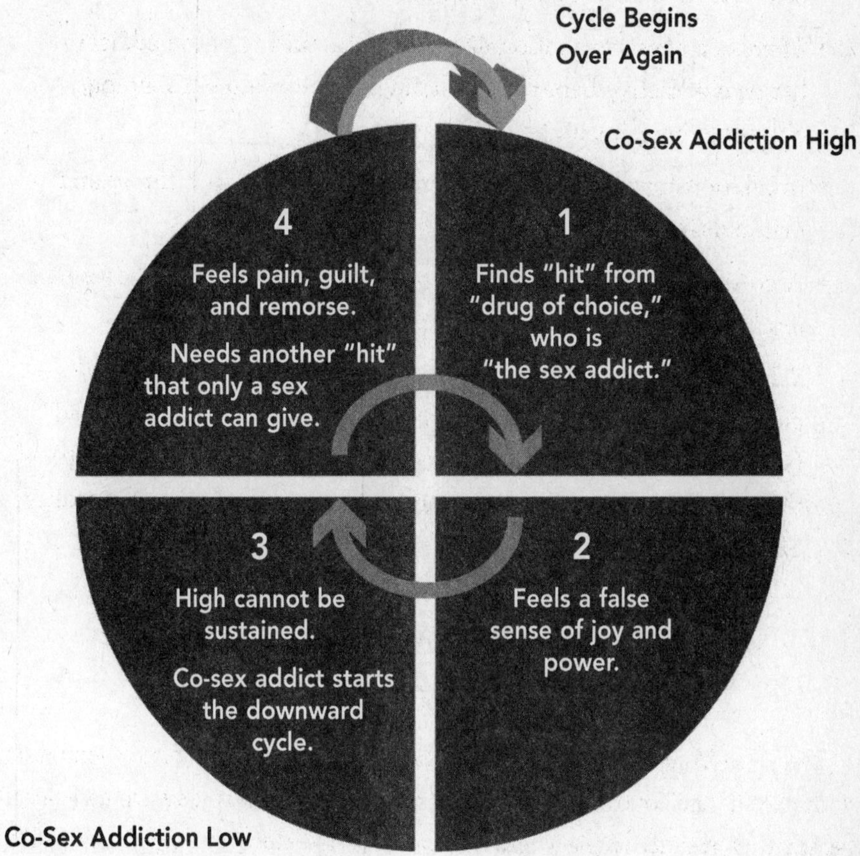

Cycle Begins
Over Again

Co-Sex Addiction High

4

Feels pain, guilt, and remorse.

Needs another "hit" that only a sex addict can give.

1

Finds "hit" from "drug of choice," who is "the sex addict."

3

High cannot be sustained.

Co-sex addict starts the downward cycle.

2

Feels a false sense of joy and power.

Co-Sex Addiction Low

It is also our experience that women in addictive relationships may have a pattern of being the "rescuers" or "caretakers" with friends and other family members. In this constant whirlwind of hearing about everyone else's drama and chaos, often the co-sex addict stays in denial about her own addictive patterns in her life and partnership. Denying our own histories and current dysfunctional relationship patterns is a common denial technique and method for minimizing and avoiding one's own painful situation. Here's an example of minimizing our own life story:

CAROLINE'S STORY

In Caroline and Wallace's relationship there was a constant drama with Caroline's sister, who was married to a man who could not hold a job and was an active alcoholic. Caroline spoke with her sister several times a week, and there was a constant litany of "Johnny's latest escapades." Caroline kept her husband apprised of all the details, and it began to fill up their communication and interactions together. When Caroline finally got into recovery for her co-sex addiction, she realized how she had kept herself occupied for years with her sister's chaotic life events as a way to avoid the pain of her own dysfunctional marriage and lack of authentic connection with her husband. She realized how much she told herself, "At least my life is not that bad, and my husband is financially responsible and provides for us." It was a way to keep from looking too closely at her own pain and her husband's secret sexual life.

Here is a classic example of sex and co-sex addiction within marriage. In Judith and Jim's story, each partner uses the other to try and fill the emptiness within.

JUDITH AND JIM'S STORY

In Judith's relationship, her partner, Jim, would often want to be sexual with her when what he really needed was some emotional closeness, encouragement, and caring. He really needed to be touched and affirmed. Without him recognizing these needs for connection and nonsexual intimacy, he would immediately attempt to be sexual with Judith.

Before Judith entered treatment and recovery for her own co-sex addiction, she would be sexual with him. This would allow her the initial *fantasy** "high" that the relationship was bonded and safe, but very soon afterward, she would feel the emptiness, anger, confusion, and fear that once again characterized her deep-down knowledge that something was not authentic in their connection.

After working through her recovery for a while, Judith was able to feel her healthy anger about being used and could say no to being sexual when genuine connection and intimacy were not present.

At the beginning, Jim's fix of sex worked, and he could leave the experience numb, having energetically transmitted those feelings onto Judith. But neediness, tension, and emptiness drove him to the next sexual hit, which started the cycle again. As is the case with addiction, after a while, the fix stopped working, and Jim made the choice to deal with his feelings and addictive behavior and began treatment.

In reality, the sexual experience for both partners was not one of closeness or genuine connection. Jim began to take responsibility for getting his emotional needs met in supportive, appropriate environments with men and with his partner, Judith. In this way, both individuals began to take care of their emotional, physical, social, and spiritual needs and were able to more readily distinguish their need and desire for healthy sexual expression.

FAMILY OF ORIGIN SETUP*
FOR CO-SEX AND SEX ADDICTION

The setup for Judith and Jim as co-sex addict and sex addict was learned in their families of origin. In addictive and dysfunctional families, the partners are inappropriately bonded, which most often refers to a child taking on a role with another adult that is most appropriately reserved for one of the adults. For example, a mother looks to her son for emotional or physical needs that she should have met with another adult. In essence, she becomes the child and her son becomes the parent. We define the term *enmeshment* as an "individual's inability to distinguish their own feelings, needs, and wants from another." The other extreme—*total disconnection**—may also occur and is defined as "the inability to relate with another person emotionally, intellectually, spiritually, or physically." Enmeshment or total disconnection occurs whenever addiction is present.

One partner in the marriage relationship/family system is seeking a sexual fix, and the other partner in the relationship is trying to control or "fix" that person and the relationship. With this addictive dynamic in full force, the children are left abandoned emotionally and/or physically, and are often pulled into an *inappropriate bond** with one or both adult addicts. With the emptiness and longing that comes from the lack of healthy emotional nurturing, they are also set up to act out addictive behaviors. The addictive cycle is repeated in an attempt to fill the emptiness.

This is an attempt of the adult addicts to get their emotional needs met because the primary adult relationship does not meet them. Both adults at this point are simply reenacting their family of origin roles and attempting to get the unmet childhood needs met. When the adults in a family system have given up themselves in pursuit of something to fill the emptiness, they are not able to be present for the emotional, spiritual, and psychological needs of their offspring. This is the intergenerational thread of addiction.

Simultaneously, they are setting up the children for their own addictive cycles of behavior. These children grow to adulthood only to repeat what was learned or what was modeled for them, that is, co-sex and sex addiction.

Giving more of Judith and Jim's story provides a good example of how the cycle of co-sex and sex addiction begins:

JUDITH AND JIM'S STORY (continued)

Judith was an *incest survivor** and learned early on that her body was for the use of the sex addict. She had not developed a healthy sense of ownership of her body and was unable to take care of herself in her sexual relationships or any relationship at all, for that matter. She could not exercise her option to say no and confused sex with love. Her inability to say no also meant she was unable to authentically say yes. Judith thought she had to be sexual in order to have a relationship or experience genuine connection.

Jim was the *hero child** and *surrogate spouse** for his mother. This meant that because of the lack of genuine connection between his father and mother, his mother turned to him to meet her needs for closeness and connection. Whenever a parent looks to a child to meet his or her needs, a setup for *emotional incest** and often physical and sexual incest takes place.

In Jim's case, the family was rigidly religious, and premarital intercourse was taboo. As the hero child in his family and the small town in which he and Judith grew up, he was considered a good catch. Jim made known his desire to marry Judith. Because of her family of origin setup for co-sex addiction, yes was her immediate answer. She did love him as much as a seventeen-year-old could. These dual setups for both of them sealed the connection between them, and they were married shortly thereafter. Although Jim did not act outside of the marriage, primarily due to the *religious addiction**/taboo of doing so in his family, he acted out inside of the marriage, consistently using sex with Judith as his primary fix. Because of her history, Judith thought it her "job" to be used sexually and to keep the marriage relationship "cemented" with sex.

FAMILY OF ORIGIN ROLES*/FAMILY ORDINALS*

A good deal of work has been done previously to assist in distinguishing the dysfunctional roles family members fall into within addictive systems. Work has also been done to assist in knowing these roles by looking at birth order within the family. Looking at the roles that family members fall into will impact one's healing and recovery. We believe those who do not look at these roles lose valuable information and depth in their development of authentic relationships.

In dysfunctional families, there is an automatic setup for family roles. These are sometimes unknowingly assigned by the parents to the children. These *assigned roles** are:

✓ *enabler**
✓ *little mother**
✓ *little princess**
✓ *assigned patient**
✓ *hero child**
✓ *little parent**
✓ *lost child**
✓ *mascot**
✓ *mediator**
✓ *offender**
✓ *scapegoat**
✓ *victim**

Some of the family of origin roles stated above have been gathered from Sharon Wegscheider-Cruse's workshops and book, *Choicemaking*.

The following automatic ordinals as referenced by Robert Sears, *American Sociological Review*, are:

✓ 1st child is father's child
✓ 2nd child is mother's child
✓ 3rd child is child of the relationship
✓ 4th child is the family standard bearer and recreates the family of origin in their adult lives

In recovery, we must look at our own roles and learn how to give them up or live them in a functional way. This must be addressed. It gives us a tremendous amount of information about ourselves and our family systems.

Because our traditional families have changed so much over the years, some of the roles and ordinals may have as well. Blended families, deaths in families, and divorced families may all change the ordinals and roles. For example, an oldest child may die, and the second child may become the primary hero in the family; or, a third-born child becomes a drug addict, leaves the family, and another child takes on that role.

We encourage individuals to be open to looking at these roles and, most importantly, honestly reviewing which roles they may have taken on. The behaviors of this role will most likely have been carried into adulthood.

EMOTIONAL ABUSE* AND INTELLECTUAL ABUSE*

When discussing *sexual abuse** and the setup for co-sex addiction, we distinguish it in many forms. Physical sexual contact with a child is the most common form of sexual abuse discussed in our culture. Emotional and intellectual sexual abuse are also very common and equally as damaging. Here are some examples of emotional and intellectual sexual abuse:

- Lack of boundaries in the home; no locked doors, no closed doors, and so on.

- Exhibitionism; adults exhibit lack of appropriate dress, robes open, sitting in underwear, and so on.

- Voyeurism; having an exaggerated interest in looking at sexual objects and/or people.

- Consistent comments about women's bodies, breasts, "getting a piece," physical attractiveness, and so on.

- Making comments about the girls'/women's bodies in the house; glaring, staring, gawking, and so on.

- Having pornography in the house in the form of magazines, videos, accessing on computers, or television.

- Sexual jokes that focus on women's bodies and sexuality or those that focus on men "getting some."

In Jim and Judith's family, Judith turned to their eldest son to try to fill some of her unmet emotional needs. She would confide in him about adult matters, unload her sadness and misery, and have conscious and sometimes unconscious expectations of him to meet her emotional needs. In Judith's case, sexual abuse did not occur with her son; however, emotional abuse did. In many cases, the adult will use the child for emotional as well as sexual gratification.

Judith's son would feel overly responsible and learned to deny his own needs, wants, and feelings in order to care for his mother. In these instances, the dynamic of reverse parenting is set into motion. The child becomes the caring parent, and the parent becomes the needy child.

This form of emotional incest is also referred to as *surrogate spouse*.* The child's emotional, sexual, spiritual, social, and physical needs are repressed, and his/her caretaking and over-responsibility is in full force. This will often lead him into his own addictive cycle of sexual/behavioral acting out, as well as substance addiction and abuse. Sometimes the addict uses substances to dull the pain of family disease along with sexual acting out.

This dynamic also takes place with a daughter and one or both parents, depending on the specific nuances in the diseased system and how it is played out in each generation. A daughter will often become a caretaker for her father's needs. She becomes the "little princess" or "little mother" to her other siblings and possibly the "mediator" between her parents. This sets her up to be a co-sex addict who focuses on the needs of the addict and how to "fix" and take care of that relationship. The "fixing" may be sexual or emotional and can become a pattern in her other relationships as well.

It is also common for the oldest or surrogate spouse child to step out of the family system, and then a younger child takes the place of the emotional partner for one of the adults. Sometimes the original surrogate spouse steps out of the dysfunctional system to break the bonds of the addictive cycle.

This was a joyful event in Judith and Jim's family, as it was the eldest son who first brought co-sex and sexual recovery and a new way of life to the family. This was the beginning of the family's journey, individually and collectively, into a new way of living through 12-step recovery.

When denial first breaks into an individual's world, and there is reflection on the family of origin and ancestry in the family, people consistently find substance and behavioral addiction in the family tree. Remember, healthy sexual and emotional behavior is learned. Addictive, dysfunctional sexual and emotional behavior is also learned. A family cycle repeats itself.

Often, families carry a strong sense of pride throughout the generations that instills an almost automatic resistance to seeing the addictive/abusive behavior of the elders. It takes great courage to see the reality of our history and those we love in their true light. There are also periods of recovery and the reclaiming of ourselves outside of the family disease where it seems almost impossible to break the generational bonds of addiction. It is true that the bonds of a family over years and years occur at a cellular and energetic level. It is only with the assistance of a Higher Power/Spiritual Source that one is able to free oneself from these addictive intergenerational family of origin behaviors.

Even in the most dysfunctional families, we find the angel or angels who give us the desire to heal and recover. These are the individuals who, despite what is going on in our immediate surroundings, offer us encouragement, acceptance, and love. For some, it is a grandparent. For others, it is a teacher, aunt, or neighbor who always made us feel welcome, understood, and safe.

It is also our belief and experience that when we are fully able to grieve the addictive patterns in our family of origin, we are then free to recognize that there were also gifts. Through our recovery, we learn to take what supports our recovery from our family of origin and to honor our heritage by learning new, more empowering behaviors for future generations. In our health and recovery, we seek to take the best from our histories and move forward to impact our family tree in its new path.

The following two charts show the ways in which our family dynamics become enmeshed or where there is total disconnection between the members. The dark outside wall describes the lack of connection and peer support for the adults and children in the family. The "wall" keeps members of the family from seeking outside professional and personal support, and keeps the dysfunction of the family system in place with the secrets of the system remaining locked inside.

Inside the dark wall, there is enmeshment and over-involvement between the adults and children, and a lack of healthy connection and alliance between the adults in the system. While healthy adult relationships require boundaries, there is also a sense of connection, sharing, and intimacy present. This behavior and recreated disconnection and enmeshment among families will be repeated intergenerationally unless *intervention** occurs, and new, healthy ways of relating are learned.

Figure 2. Recovering Healthy Family and Intergenerational Relationships

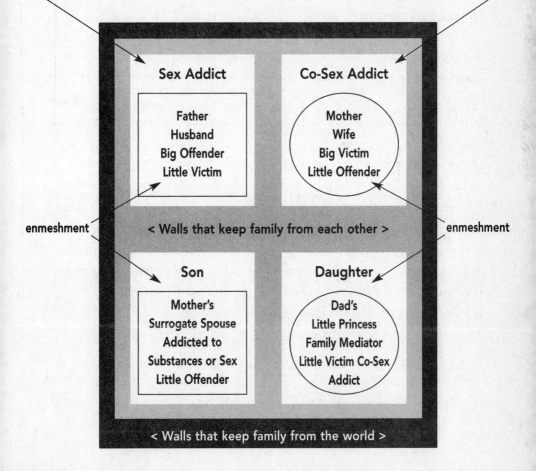

- Leaves family to act out with affairs, emotional affairs, fantasy, uses partner sexually, and/or compulsive mastur-bation, etc.

- Leaves family to act out with emotional and/or physical affairs, uses children emo-tionally, becomes sexually anorexic and/or promiscuous, becomes obsessed with control and/or fixing, etc.

Sex Addict

Father
Husband
Big Offender
Little Victim

Co-Sex Addict

Mother
Wife
Big Victim
Little Offender

enmeshment

< Walls that keep family from each other >

enmeshment

Son

Mother's
Surrogate Spouse
Addicted to
Substances or Sex
Little Offender

Daughter

Dad's
Little Princess
Family Mediator
Little Victim Co-Sex
Addict

< Walls that keep family from the world >

**Figure 3. Recovering Healthy Family and
Intergenerational Relationships**

Sex Addict	Co-Sex Addict
• Finds healthy connection to co-sex addict	• Finds healthy connection to sex addict
• Stays in family after therapy	• Learns healthy sex
• Attends 12-step meetings	• Available to sex addict and children
• Practices healthy sex	• Joins 12-step program
• Has spiritual connection	• Has spiritual connection
Son	**Daughter**
• Free to leave old roles	• Finds own recovery
• Seeks authentic relationship	• Free to have authentic relationships
• Finds Higher Power	• Finds Higher Power
• Looks at his addictions	• Has spiritual connection

All are free to have healthy, authentic relationships outside the family.
All find healthy, authentic connection with one another within the family.

HITTING A CO-SEX ADDICTION BOTTOM

Hitting bottom in one's disease may look similar to another's and may also have very unique qualities. This is one story of a woman hitting her co-sex addiction bottom.

BELL'S STORY

Hitting a co-sex addiction bottom for Bell meant having feelings and memories from her abuse history that were so disturbing she was ready to do anything to clear up her mind. Bleeps of things from the past, even scores of years ago, kept creeping into her mind. Almost as quickly as they would creep in, her denial and protective defense mechanisms would take over. She returned to her strange acting-out behaviors to keep the memories out of consciousness. In co-sex addiction, these strange acting-out behaviors included getting a hit from her drugs of choice. These were the sex addicts in her life: husband, sons, and male friends.

In the beginning, a phone call from her drug of choice would alter her mind so that the memories of early abuse would once again recede to the depths of her consciousness. The best choice for a hit was Bell's behavior of spending hours "fixing" those addicts who would then try to fill her "needs." If her husband needed a fix, she would fix his need with sex. Maybe his work felt overwhelming to him. When she would see this fear of failure at work, *rage,** and sadness at not feeling good enough for the task, he could temporarily get "fixed" in bed. Most of the uncomfortable feelings Art would have, Bell knew she could temporarily fix in bed—only "temporary" is the clue that this was addiction and an addictive pattern.

Soon he would hit another bottom, and she would have the need to fix him again. This was her addictive behavior: giving sex and romance, being told she was beautiful, a good wife and mother, and that she was smart. This was her temporary fix. Sometimes what she got instead of a fix was shame. She would begin to feel used and would then be unable to perform sexually. This caused her husband to rage and accuse her that it was her inability to perform that was causing all this trouble. This was a merry-go-round of a marriage.

What began to happen is that the bleeps of childhood abuse memories were getting triggered in her marriage. These repressed memories of childhood felt the same as the feelings of being used in her marriage with her primary addict. In other words, having sex with her husband—being used to fix him—would trigger memories from the original sexual abuse in her family. This was an inevitable step to her hitting bottom. Bell would then disassociate and lose all sexual feelings. Her body was remembering the sexual abuse of a little girl, and that little girl did not want sex then or now. Her reality was damaged by those early years of abuse by those who should have been caring for her and loving her. Instead, she received sex, not love, caring, or protection. Bell could feel this damage inside of her, even though she did not have memories of the actual abuse that led to her feeling crazy. Her only relief from "feeling crazy" were the occasional bleeps of repressed childhood memories that were becoming conscious. At these times, she would wonder, *Could this kind of sex that is happening now—that feels like it is not about me—have happened before?*

Bell would then have the need to find someone who would not interact with her sexually, but would tell her what she wanted to hear: how wonderful, good, smart, unique, sexy, and beautiful she was. Even though these things may have been true about Bell, it was her temporary fix to fill her emptiness inside. Because of the ways Bell was abused, she did not have self-esteem and worthiness and needed to get her fix from sex addicts. This was the only way she knew to try to fill the emptiness and pain inside.

Co-sex addiction codependency is about the need for fixing another so that he/she can fix you. The only real fix for Bell was with a sex addict who would initially make her feel wonderful, and then tear her down with shame and similar messages from childhood, especially that she was a bad person. As she was hitting bottom and no longer fixing her husband, she was feeling like a bad wife for not providing all the sex her husband wanted. The shaming from her husband began to feel familiar to her. It was the familiar cycle of her childhood abuse: being used sexually, getting her temporary fix of giving sex and being told she was okay, and then the shaming and blaming beginning again.

Bell found other relationships outside of her marriage. This happened as she sought someone who would "love" her and not expect her to be sexual. In Bell's case, a gay man filled the bill in her life. He told her how beautiful and sexy she was and claimed that she was the best friend he had ever had. Every "hook" that Bell wanted was initially received in this relationship. What she finally realized was that this con man, too, was using her. He wanted another man over whom she had some influence. Once again, Bell was being used, and the cycle of lies was repeated again. She was trying to get her fix, but was instead experiencing more and more shame. This led Bell to hit bottom.

The relationship with the gay man finally stopped fixing her, and Bell retreated and regressed into her past abuse. Bleeps of the childhood memories begin to appear again. She kept trying to get the hit and keep the memories repressed by fixing her husband sexually and her gay friend emotionally. She began to find there was no relief or fix any longer. She was in more physical and emotional pain and shame. This deep emotional pain was related to the feelings from childhood when she wanted to be connected, loved, and cared for, but only received abuse from her father and brother. Finally, someone in Bell's life saw the pain she was in and helped her by contacting a therapist. This therapist sent Bell to treatment. She did not know anything about treatment or therapy, but because she hurt so badly, she was willing to do anything to get out of pain.

In recovery, Bell now knows that hitting bottom in co-sex addiction and detoxing from co-sexually addictive relationships can be as physically, emotionally, mentally, and spiritually devastating and powerful as detoxing from any other drug or behavior. Upon leaving the sex addicts and co-sex addiction cycles in her life and going to treatment, she had physical symptoms and hallucinations just like a narcotic addict in withdrawal. She found that treatment had many paradoxes that included horror and happiness. She had to delve into the pain to experience authentic joy. Also, having clarity about her past abuse has given her the ability to live fully in her present life.

Bell finally understands that her troubled life was about repression of memories of childhood abuse and that this was part of her co-sex addiction. Her need and sickness in co-sex addiction were to find a sex addict who she could fix. In her disease, this gave her the temporary fix of feeling worthy, needed, and loved. With recovery and treatment, Bell discovered that her worthiness and value must come from within and from her Higher Power. She began her journey of looking deep inside of herself.

First, she had to truly feel her feelings from her childhood—including the horrors—rather than trying to fix the pain. Treatment and 12-step programs gave her a safe place where she was gently helped into reality and could grieve her abusive history. She received the message in treatment that when you feel your feelings, reality will be yours and a new life can begin. Twenty-eight days in the desert for treatment was significant in beginning her journey of recovery, which continued in her 12-step program after she returned home. Bell returned home feeling her feelings and knowing she had much more work to do to recover her memories of abuse that had initially set her up for co-sex addiction. Her path was attending Co-Sex Addicts Anonymous meetings and attendance at many workshops on family of origin healing and sexual abuse. She found that what she was told in treatment—that if she attended 12-step recovery programs and continued to do her *step work** and writing, she would find peace—was true. Her journey to authentic relationships and *powerful serenity** had begun.

SOCIETY AS THE ENABLER OF CO-SEX ADDICTION

We've discussed how families set up children to look outside of themselves for fulfillment, causing addictive patterns to begin. We also believe our culture is a breeding ground for co-sex and sex addiction.

Little girls are conditioned from a very young age to "be nice" and "look pretty." The focus in our culture is on a particular body type, and how one looks is highly regarded. Plastic surgery is commonplace in our culture, and there is little support for honoring the wisdom of women or the elderly.

Television ads, movies, and even billboards also display our culture's attitude toward sexuality. A mother recently shared with us a large advertisement on a billboard for a tanning salon that had a teenage girl saying, "I know what the boys like." News and television networks are known in the media industry for requiring women to lose weight to fit the distorted and unrealistic image of how a woman "should" look.

Inner beauty and character should be the focus of attention instead. A person's spirit and who they really are inside, rather than the outside appearance, are a more valid measuring stick of value. When appearance is the focal point, there is a setup and drive inside little girls growing into adolescence to find their own approval and value from the culture, primarily from men. Men decide, for the most part, what is beautiful, what is marketed, and what gets the most attention.

Research indicates that during adolescent years, IQ scores of young girls decline noticeably, especially in the area of math and science. Up until this point, young girls consistently excel compared to their male counterparts. We believe it is during this time that there is a huge shift in the focus on intellectual achievement. Their outer appearance and attention to co-gender relationships become most important. An argument could be made that, here again, the need for approval from boys or men has become the primary drive, and it is hard to get approval from someone you are smarter than or beating in the spelling bee.

In this area, once more, our culture and family of origin messages may be taking over. How you look, how "nice" and "sweet" and "sexy" you act, make the difference in terms of the attention you get. High achievement and intellect in young girls do not have the same high value.

Over the past few years, national news services have been reporting on the phenomenon of young people acting out sexually in the area of oral sex. Data are being collected and recorded, and the numbers are staggering. Adolescent boys and girls come together socially and engage in oral sex. Few of these young people make a distinction between the experience of oral sex and kissing. We believe this reflects how inundated our culture is with casual sex and the confusion our society has about genuine intimacy. This, combined with a young girl's drive to fill her own internal emptiness with male approval, leads her to do whatever it takes to be accepted, desirable, and validated. This includes having oral sex wherever and whenever it is requested by the boys in their social circles.

For young boys, locker room talk has already begun. They have also been inundated with messages saying masculinity is about "getting some." This is part of their "sex addict" setup: getting a fix from sex or a sexual act, even if there is the belief that there is nothing intimate or sexual about it. Movies, television, the music industry, and advertising reinforce this mistaken notion about relationships. The collapse of intimacy and sex, and the lack of distinguishing between the two, occur over and over again. There is little guidance or modeling from our culture or our families about connecting authentically with one another or distinguishing between sexuality and intimacy. When young people have been taught how to value themselves internally, as well as share their feelings and experiences with one another, there is a sense of fulfillment and joy inside. They come together to express themselves with age-appropriate activities and to have fun in the process. The drive to act out sexually, give one's body to another for approval, or fill the emptiness inside with sexual activities is absent, and healthy age-appropriate interactions are present.

KATH'S STORY

One afternoon I received a call from my daughter's school. There was an emergency meeting called that evening at the school with other parents regarding an "incident" that had come to the attention of the school counselor and administration. That evening I learned that a dozen or more seventh- and eighth-grade students from my daughter's school were meeting on a regular basis at our local movie theater and engaging in oral sex. I knew my daughter was going to afternoon matinees and meeting her friends there, but I had no idea that this activity was taking place. Upon interviewing my daughter about the incident, she said, "Everyone is doing it, Mom, and there is really no difference between it and kissing." I was beyond shocked and immediately made an appointment with a counselor and our doctor.

My daughter and I began to communicate more, and I learned how to express my own feelings and be more available to her. I began to share some of my own challenges at her age, and with counseling she began to see how her behavior was a reflection of her own loneliness and anger that she was carrying inside. The counseling also assisted her in realizing her anger and sadness about the lack of relationship and healthy connection that she missed with her father since our divorce. She began to grieve this loss, and even though her dad lived in another state, she reached out to him more, and their relationship took on a more positive quality.

We also met with our family physician who spoke very frankly about sexually transmitted diseases (STDs) and how they are contracted. My daughter had no idea what she was setting herself up for and the possible consequences of her actions. It was a shocking and jarring experience for both of us, but because of counseling and our willingness to get help, it has been the catalyst to a real relationship with my daughter.

2

Healthy
Family Systems

*I*n healthy family systems, each individual's needs, thoughts, feelings, and contributions are equally valued. The adults are able to identify and acknowledge their feelings (anger, sadness, joy, fear, guilt, etc.) and model how to share them in a healthy and respectful way. There is no need to use mood-altering drugs or other addictive behaviors. People have and express their emotions in healthy and appropriate ways so there is no need to escape the dynamics of the family. Individuals are able to be themselves and express themselves freely, and the family system is a place of safety, connection, and nurturing.

Individuals who have the ability to connect with and embrace their feelings are able to identify needs and wants and share feelings in the family. From this foundation of emotional connection and sharing, intimacy is created. When feelings are shared authentically between partners, a healthy, trustful bond is established. From this bond, the adults are able to take responsibility for being emotionally available to the needs of the children.

Appropriate bonds are created between family members when the necessary boundaries are modeled and taught. Individuals are protected against

31

enmeshment and/or abandonment. Each adult partner also has the ability to reach out for appropriate emotional/spiritual support outside of the primary relationship and/or marriage. This support nurtures them individually in a healthy way without interfering with the bond of the primary relationship. It is also gender appropriate for women to receive support and connection with other women and men to receive some support and healthy emotional connection with other men. Same-gender support is especially important with the co-sex addict and sex addict, because part of their disease is to attempt to receive connection and support from the opposite sex.

Out of the intimate relationship and bond between the adults in the family system, authentic relationships occur, thus giving birth to individual personal power. This also leads to powerful serenity. Below is an example of healthy adult bonding in a family.

JIM AND JUDITH'S STORY AFTER RECOVERY

After Judith and Jim started 12-step recovery and family of origin healing work for their co-sex and sex addiction, they were able to communicate their feelings, needs, and wants directly to each other. Most importantly, Jim and Judith gained the ability to distinguish their individual needs for emotional nurturing and nonsexual affection. They no longer confused sex for love or sexual connection for nonsexual and emotional nurturing. This then transferred to their ability to relate healthfully to their children.

Megan, their daughter, had been consistently pulled into her parents' relationship. Judith would confide in Megan, and Megan would try to mediate their difficulties. This third-party interaction is called *triangulation*.*

When Judith and Jim began to see this dysfunctional dynamic in the family system, they no longer used their daughter to assist in mediating their arguments. They also stopped sharing their individual complaints about the other spouse with her. When Judith and Jim noticed Megan's resistance to giving up this role, they actually sat her down and "fired" her as mediator. Megan's facial expression was one of relief and joy. This relieved her of the burden and responsibility of taking care of her parents' relationship. It freed her up to focus on her own life and her own age-appropriate emotional, physical, sexual, social, and spiritual development.

As Jim and Judith continued to nurture their own emotional needs and develop genuine emotional intimacy with each other, their sexual expression became more vibrant as well. The sexual relationship became an expression of their love and respect for each other rather than a venue for fixing, avoiding, or using each other. They no longer used their sexual relating inappropriately.

Sometimes in families, this formal ritual is necessary in order to give full permission to the individuals in the system to give up their dysfunctional roles. When taking on dysfunctional roles in a diseased system, one does so to "fit in" and survive within the family. Even when we realize our behaviors are harmful and ineffective, we are often challenged in giving them up and changing our habits. The roles and ways we fit into a dysfunctional family were set in place to survive and keep the system alive. Consistent recovery, the practicing of new behaviors, and a connection with a Higher Power and healthy support group such as Co-Sex Addicts Anonymous and 12-step groups are necessary to break these old patterns of bondage and create new, fulfilling ways of relating based within freedom and choice. It is often helpful to support 12-step recoveries by seeing a qualified therapist who understands co-sex and sex addiction and family of origin work.

True intimacy is the foundation for healthy sex. Intimacy begins with the recognition of one's responsibility for one's own feelings, needs, and desires rather than focusing on the feelings, needs, and desires of one's partner. True intimacy also means focusing on oneself and taking responsibility for emotional, sexual, and spiritual fulfillment, not thinking fulfillment occurs through another person.

We come into recovery believing that intimacy and sex are the same and/or that someone wanting us sexually means they love us. After recovery, we begin to learn the meaning of authentic emotional intimacy. We also learn to distinguish between using sex to fill the emptiness inside versus genuine sexual expression that occurs within an authentic, intimate relationship.

CHARACTERISTICS OF DYSFUNCTIONAL SYSTEMS VS. CHARACTERISTICS OF FUNCTIONAL SYSTEMS

Emotionally Dysfunctional System

- Feelings are not allowed or expressed appropriately.

- Violence and rage are acted out in the system by some, while others are the victims of the violence and rage, or there is *silent rage.**

- One or both of the parents are inappropriately bonded with the child and not bonded with each other.

- There are secrets, a lack of open communication, and simmering tension constantly in the family, as though everyone is waiting for the "other shoe to drop."

Emotionally Functional System

- Feelings of hurt, sadness, joy, fear, and anger are expressed appropriately, respectfully, and openly. These feelings are acknowledged by others in the family.

- There are no offenders or victims. Each person deals responsibly with their own feelings and behaviors and allows others to do the same. The family system holds appropriate accountability for each individual's behavior. Any abusive behavior is confronted immediately with appropriate consequences given.

- When inappropriate behavior or old dysfunctional roles emerge, the functional system empowers individuals to confront these behaviors and then move on.

Physically Dysfunctional System

- There are no physical boundaries, and privacy is nonexistent.

- Enmeshment is present. The individual's need for privacy and confidentiality is not valued.

- Rage is acted out by hitting, beating, pushing, and other physical expressions.

Physically Functional System

- People have their own space.

- Closed and locked doors are respected.

- Everyone has a right to privacy.

- Individuals in the family have a right to their own boundaries and the right to engage in appropriate touching or not.

- When anger is present, it is expressed in nonviolent ways with appropriate consequences.

Intellectually Dysfunctional System

- Children are brainwashed by the adults in the system, and individual perspectives are not encouraged.

- Most issues fall into a black/white, right/wrong category.

- The "head" of the family makes all of the decisions for everyone, and autonomy or free expression is not allowed or valued.

Intellectually Functional System

- Individual opinions are encouraged and respected.
- Each person in the family is encouraged to make their own decisions and solve their own problems, with guidance and support when necessary.
- Diversity and individuality are valued.

Spiritually Dysfunctional System

- Usually "God" in the family is one of the adults, and everything revolves around that person.
- The thoughts, actions, and practices of the adults are rubber-stamped and rarely questioned.
- Self-expression, creativity, passion, and joy are replaced with rigid religious rituals.

Spiritually Functional System

- A connection to a spiritual source is modeled by the adults, and a sincere and unique expression of faith is encouraged.
- The individuals in the system have their own passions, creative expressions, joys, and so on, which are honored and encouraged as a deep expression of their being.
- Spiritual reality and connecting with a spiritual source are daily practices individually and as a family.

Sexually Dysfunctional System

- Sex is about selfish gratification and leaves people feeling empty, used, and/or alienated.

- Sex is a taboo subject that is not openly discussed. There is overt and covert objectification woven into the fabric of daily conversation, that is, sexual jokes, comments about women, explicit pictures displayed, and so on.

- Sexual dysfunction means there are no boundaries. For example, emotional or physical incest, exhibitionism, objectification, voyeurism, and so on exist in varying degrees.

Sexually Functional System

- The pleasures and joys of the body are accepted and celebrated with appropriate boundaries.

- Concerns, questions, and information requested by the young children within the family are addressed and responded to within the context of age-appropriate information.

- The parent/parents in the family model appropriate boundaries concerning their own sexuality and sexual expression.

- Sexual expression is valued as an intimate experience of one's deepest spiritual being.

3

The Core of
Co-Sex Addiction

The core of co-sex addiction is rooted in being set up as a victim. One of the first pieces of work that we do in recovery from co-sex addiction concerns seeing our setup as victims and our re-creation of that dynamic in adult life. As children, we did not have the power of choice to avoid being set up and victimized. As adults, we begin to see our part in recreating this victim/offender dynamic. Once we see this, we begin to learn new behaviors and exercise our power of choice in relationships with others.

In our original addictive family of origin dynamics, there is typically one individual who acts in the primary offender role, and the other members are set up as victims. This primary offender/addict is most likely the man or husband in the "traditional" family system. (This offender/victim dynamic, of course, takes place in same-gender relationships as well.) The woman in this "traditional" family system is set up as a victim. She carries the shame of the offender who, while in addiction, is unable to feel appropriate remorse for his acting out and/or abusive behavior.

The mother's addiction is also one of enabling, co-sex addiction, and co-dependency. She stays busy covering up, tolerating, denying, and pretending that "all is well." She models the victim/enabler.

In a dysfunctional family, all the children become victims themselves, until they reach a certain age and developmental stage. At this time, they will either remain victims by continuing to be set up as victims or move into the offender role by victimizing others. This victimization often takes place within the family with other siblings. The evidence is now overwhelming that sex offenders were consistently victimized themselves as children.

Jill's Story

In Jill's family, her older brother, John, was sexually abused by their father, the "primary" offender in the family. The father forced the son (victim) to perform oral sex. Later on, John then sexually abused his sister, Jill, the "new" victim. Here we see that the victim becomes the offender, and the offender (brother) finds a new victim (sister). The sexual abuse continued for several years until John left for college.

Because of the lack of healthy emotional nurturing and connection in the family, his leaving felt like abandonment to Jill. Even though their connection was horrifically dysfunctional and victimizing, for Jill it was the only connection she experienced within her abusive, emotionally cold, and empty family. This is often the case with sexual abuse victims.

Here we see that Jill's setup was to be sexually abused by an older person and then physically abandoned. Jill then acted out this family dynamic and her role by choosing a boyfriend who was several years older and having him immediately go off to college, leaving her behind. She promised to be faithful only to him. Because of the family setup, Jill began to look for nonsexual male friendships to fill the void of the brother she longed for. However, because of the sexual abuse and her setup, she attracted men who were initially kind to her and would gain her trust, and then she would be date-raped and abused, just like her brother had done for years.

Later in the book, we will write extensively on shame, but a brief explanation will do well in this context. When one is victimized as a child and is set up to take on the shame of the offender(s), often the only option is to recreate this dynamic as an adult, since this is the only system the victim knows. When a woman is physically, emotionally, and/or sexually used in her family of origin, she carries the shame for her abuser(s). The abuser/offender is unable to feel remorse, guilt, or appropriate sorrow for his inappropriate behavior. When this occurs, the energy must go somewhere, and the victim, with no boundaries, takes it in and believes she is at fault. The guilt and remorse of the offender, which he denies, becomes shame in the victim, and she carries the shame for the offense. The deep sense of worthlessness and the feeling that she is deserving of abuse is the shame that becomes manifested in the victim.

The dynamic of shame is the need for the victim to have an identity. She would rather take on the shame ("this is all my fault") than be nothing or have to admit how unsafe she is with abusive caregivers. To take on this identity of always being at fault is the least frightening and painful of all options. This is a family of origin dysfunction and also the way that a child thinks. In her brilliance and determination to survive, a child takes on whatever beliefs are necessary to survive the situation: "At least I know who I am and have an identity, even if I am 'a piece of shit'; I deserve this behavior," and/or "my body is a tool." Taking on this identity provides a false sense of security, and this is better than having no sense of security or admitting how dangerous an environment really is. This is what children do. Generally, when we grow into adulthood, we repeat what we have learned as children. This re-creation most often happens unconsciously. A major part of our recovery is bringing into awareness these unconscious beliefs and taking conscious action to share them.

Only intervention can jar us enough to hit our bottom, rethink these dynamics learned in childhood, and risk new behaviors. These new behaviors dramatically contradict the shame, our familiar perspective, and beliefs. We begin to re-create our relationships and how we interact with others. We are no longer willing to carry the shame or guilt of others' behavior. We begin to take responsibility for our own behavior, nothing more and nothing less, according to our own value system identified in recovery. The victim is free to begin to live a shame-free life with boundaries and in alignment with her own value system identified in recovery.

When and if the offender responds to intervention and gets into recovery, he will begin to feel his own remorse and guilt for his actions. The offender will hopefully remain in recovery as well and begin to live according to his value system also. Remember, shame is what is done to us. Guilt is what we have done ourselves.

JILL'S STORY (continued)

After repeated sexual, physical, and emotional abuse by her brother, Jill internalized his shame and began to feel "like a piece of shit." Often John would hit her, push her down, and call her names, such as "fatty" and "ugly," which she internalized as well. His shaming behavior served a dual purpose: John did not have to feel any of his own feelings, and he kept Jill feeling so bad about herself that she would never confront him or speak up about the abuse. John did not feel any remorse or guilt for his behavior, so Jill took it on in the form of internalized shame.

When Jill became a mother and wife, she became the victim in her marriage and the offender with her children. Jill provided sex on demand to her sex-addict husband and used physical means to discipline her children. She was unable to model healthy behavior for her children and thus re-created the dynamic she learned in childhood in various forms. In treatment for co-sex addiction, Jill was able to recognize her own sexual abuse, and her children learned about the dynamic of sexual abuse and how it played out in their current family. Over time in recovery, the family learned new behaviors and began to address the dysfunctional, shame-filled dynamic that had been modeled and learned by them.

Unless intervention occurs, individuals continue to act out the dysfunctional roles that were learned in their addictive family systems. They recreate this dynamic of offender and victim in their adult lives. If authentic relationships are to be realized, individuals must distinguish their own learned addictive behaviors. Learning new behaviors that empower individuals to be in authentic relationships based on equality, respect, and mutual support is the outcome of 12-step recovery. This process does not come easily, however, as the experience of breaking through the denial and grieving the losses from the abusive setups in our families of origin is painful.

BIG OFFENDER/LITTLE VICTIM AND BIG VICTIM/LITTLE OFFENDER

We would now like to introduce the concept of Big Offender/little victim and Big Victim/little offender. Without recovery intervention, this dynamic occurs:

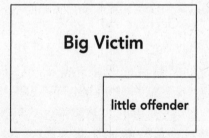

Every human being has both dynamics in their repertoire of dysfunctional and obsessive/compulsive behaviors. When one is set up in their family of origin to be a victim, it becomes the primary role they re-create in their adult lives. When one is set up to be offender in their family of origin, the primary role they re-create in their adult lives is that of an offender.

Each of these primary addictive roles has a secondary addictive/dysfunctional role as well. We refer to these as Big Offender/little victim and Big

Victim/little offender. One who is consistently being victimized will eventually act out as an offender. The wife/woman who is in the victim role with her husband will often act out by victimizing her children. She then becomes the offender. The primary addict/offender/husband in the family will also act out from a victim role.

> EXAMPLE: Jeffrey, when home, raged and acted out the offender role with his wife and children. At work, however, his secretary would fly into rages, often shaming him and yelling. He tolerated this behavior for years, even though he had the power to fire her. He remained in the "little victim" role with her. For Jeffrey, this was a re-created dynamic from his family of origin and his relationship with his mother.

As co-sex addicts, it is often difficult to acknowledge our part in the dysfunctional behavior of the little offender. We do not like to admit that we hurt people in the way that we were most often victimized. This is an important part of our recovery.

However, one's primary role of Big Offender and Big Victim must be addressed *first* before looking at the secondary dysfunctional roles of little victim and little offender. *We cannot stress this point enough.* There is an order and structure of recovery from co-sex and sex addiction. We must follow this structure to avoid getting stuck in a particular stage in the recovery process.

When your primary setup in your family of origin is to be a victim, this must be addressed in recovery *first*. The little offender role is secondary for the co-sex addict. When the primary dysfunctional setup in your family of origin is the offender role, you must address this behavior in recovery *first*. The little victim role is secondary.

Oftentimes for the victim, being an offender is associated with being powerful and can become a block to recovery from co-sex addiction. We do not want to admit we are victims. Since being a victim is our primary pattern of relating in the world, embracing it and coming out of denial leaves us in unfamiliar territory. It is sometimes easier to focus on our little offender rather than our primary victim and fully taking responsibility for our lives.

When we take a shortcut in our recovery from co-sex addiction and focus too early on the little offender secondary dysfunctional role, we sabotage our recovery by remaining stuck in a cycle of shame, denial, and addictive behavior. Oftentimes the preference is to look at the little offender behavior, since as co-sex addicts we become so accustomed to carrying and feeling shame. When we are acting out by hurting others in ways we have been hurt, we can easily feed the shame we already carry for our offenders.

Some of the ways co-sex addicts might act out the little offender role include verbally raging, physically disciplining, shaming, harsh punishments, overcontrolling, and so on. These behaviors are not to be confused with healthy anger, which is a necessary tool in recovery from co-sex/victim addiction.

Just as often, for the offender, being a victim is a way of denying the degree of his own abusive and offensive behavior. Here the sex addict does not want to admit he is an offender. Because this is his primary pattern of relating in the world, embracing it and coming out of denial leaves him in uncharted territory as well.

It is sometimes easier for the Big Offender to focus on his little victim than his primary offender. It is challenging for him to take full responsibility and acknowledge his abusive behavior. Sometimes sex addicts will own that they are co-sex addicts in this dynamic. We also see co-sex addicts wanting to go to other 12-step programs. In our opinion, this is an example of not dealing with the primary addictive dynamic.

EXAMPLE: Eve attended Sex and Love Addicts Anonymous meetings for years, as well as Sex Addicts Anonymous meetings, and called herself a sex addict. Her acting out with men in casual sexual relationships continued, and she remained in a lot of pain. She finally began to see a therapist who insisted that she do family of origin work, in which she finally remembered that she was sexually abused by a neighbor as a young girl. As she continued to do her grief work* concerning this abuse and own her co-sex addiction and the way in which she was victimized, she began to attend Co-Sex Addicts Anonymous meetings and stopped acting out sexually. Eve realized that maintaining that she was a sex addict and not looking at the original victimization and abuse she experienced was a way to avoid the pain and keep her in denial. Her recovery from co-sex addiction is going strong today, and she is currently in a committed relationship with a man who is also working a 12-step program.

Looking at the pain under the shame is very difficult. Therefore, there is a pull early on in 12-step recovery for a co-sex addiction to deny her victim role and overly focus on her little offender behaviors. She may attempt to attend meetings for sex addicts.

Offenders/sex addicts may also avoid their pain-filled identity and avoid dealing with the shame of their offender behavior by focusing on being a victim. They might focus on their victimization rather than fully embracing their primary role as Big Offender and acknowledging the degree of hurt and harm imposed on others. This may occur in the form of him attending COSA meetings. Thus, both are trying to avoid their real work and "switching realities."

EXAMPLE: Sarah and David's relationship is an example of being set up as Big Victim and staying stuck by overfocusing or focusing too early on the little offender. Sarah explains, "When I was married, my husband would be verbally abusive. When there was a fight or disagreement, his energy level would rise, and he would start to verbally attack me. He would say things like, 'What the fuck is your problem?'

Or 'Fuck you!' or 'You are just a bitch!' At first, I would go into shock. I would try to convince him that his language and behavior were inappropriate. I would try to figure out what I had done to provoke him. I was taking responsibility for his abusive behavior. I was the victim. Later, I started to fight back. I would start screaming and telling him to 'Shut the fuck up' or say 'Fuck you' back. What he would then do was take those few moments when I fought back and turn me into the offender. He would talk only about how verbally and physically abusive I was and that I was the offender. He would totally deny responsibility for his abusive behavior and his part in the abusive cycle.

"After months of living like this, I went to a meeting at our local women's shelter for abused women. I was carrying all the guilt for my behavior (from my little offender) and my Big Victim was carrying all of his shame from his Big Offender, who was denying his responsibility for his own behavior. His abusive behavior extended into verbal, emotional, physical, and financial arenas.

"While I was sharing in the meeting and talking about the few times I was offensive instead of focusing on his behavior, a woman spoke up and said, 'When you are beat up again and again, physically, verbally, emotionally, and financially, eventually you are going to fight back.' This really helped me to see how once again I was stuck in the victim role. This man was clearly in the offender role.

"When I was talking in the women's shelter meeting, I inappropriately focused my attention on the few times I would verbally strike back at my husband rather than the details of his constantly abusive behavior. In other words, my Big Victim was taking responsibility as being the offender in the relationship rather than focusing on his

Big Offender. My part was overfocusing on my little offender and denying how my Big Victim was carrying the shame for his Big Offender. I was stuck in being a victim and enabling his offender behavior."

FANTASY THINKING AS PART OF THE DISEASE

Infatuation or *fantasy thinking** is a big part of the disease of co-sex addiction and sex addiction. In our self-help and recovery circles, this has been referred to as "love addiction," "romance addiction," "relationship addiction," "fantasy," and "co-sex addiction." All of these addictive patterns of thinking or acting relate to living in a fantasy about relationships. We believe all of these distinctions fall under the category of co-sex addiction. It doesn't necessarily matter what it is called; the solution is the same.

All addicts are driven by a similar emptiness inside that may be temporarily relieved through a variety of fixes. In their disease, sex addicts believe sex will fix anything, and they use it to provide a temporary relief to avoid experiencing their feelings and the emptiness inside. Co-sex addicts will have sex because in their fantasy thinking, they believe this will cement the relationship. They use the fantasy of the relationship to fill their emptiness.

When the co-sex addict or sex addict hits bottom and comes face-to-face with her or his need for help, an opportunity for a new way of living in recovery emerges. The co-sex addict or sex addict no longer experiences the temporary relief of addictive behavior. She or he can no longer live in the fantasy that sex or a relationship will fill the emptiness inside.

Solutions for both addicts are spiritual in nature and begin by accepting the pain/emptiness inside. In recovery, we begin to fill this hole inside with spiritual connection. This is the major focus in 12-step programs. We have learned in our recovery program that the solution is spiritual. We believe that family of origin/grief work is the essential partner that will create the space for the Spiritual Solution.

This spiritual focus teaches us to first develop an authentic connection with a spiritual source, which is often referred to as a "Higher Power" in our 12-step programs. Simultaneously, we begin to create and develop an authentic connection with ourselves. Last, with the resources we have, we are able to create and experience authentic relationships with other human beings.

4

Shame Versus Empowerment

*A*ddiction and addictive behavior of any sort is fueled by shame, and shame is characteristic of the dysfunctional family system. Shame, for the purpose of our discussion, is defined as the feeling and sense that we are not enough, something is wrong with us, people might find out, we just don't deserve to live, and so on. We believe that this is about what has "happened to us" and how we were hurt and victimized in our families. This abusive setup in our family of origin causes us "energetically" to carry the shame of the offenders who use and abuse us. We act out this shame in ways similar to the original abuse.

Guilt, for the purposes of our discussion, is defined as the feeling we have when we realize that we have contradicted our own value system. It is the feeling that has us take responsibility for our behavior. Guilt is a guide that supports us in staying aligned with our healthy values and gives us information. It reminds us to take responsibility for our behavior, make amends when necessary, and take actions to build our self-esteem and keep our lives going in the new direction we have chosen in recovery.

As co-sex addicts set up to be victims, we begin to carry the shame of our abusers. The sense of shame replaces the gift of self-empowerment and healthy self-care. The cycle of shame begins. Once we are in this cycle of behavior, our innate sense of healthy self-care and empowerment becomes more and more diminished as we take on more and more shame of the abusers in our lives.

Lillian's Story

After Lillian started her recovery from co-sex addiction, she retrieved memories of being sexually abused as a young girl by her father. He was a plastic surgeon, so on the outside, to the social community, he was well respected, accomplished, and "looked good." At home, however, he would terrorize Lillian and engage her physically, emotionally, and spiritually in degrading sexual behavior, all of which was a "secret" to family and friends.

After the abuse started, she would feel shame, like it was her fault or she had done something to cause the abuse, and her father acted shamelessly, continuing with the abuse and threatening her with keeping it silent. Lillian carried his shame.

In junior high, she began acting out the abuse and the shame she felt by sexual activity with high-school boys and older men. This was really an unconscious "reenactment" of the sexual abuse and torment of her childhood. Eventually, Lillian became a topless dancer and prostitute. She consistently prostituted herself with men twenty-plus years older than her and allowed herself to be used by them. This was similar to her relationship with her father.

After recovery, she began to talk about what happened to her by her father and the shame that she carried about his abuse of her. This was not her shame but her father's, which she carried from his abuse of her. As Lillian continued to do more family of origin work and used Co-Sex Addicts Anonymous 12-step tools, she understood her acting out behavior as a consequence of carrying her father's shame for his abuse of her. She was able to begin the grieving process, feel her feelings, and have appropriate anger and boundaries with her dysfunctional and abusive family of origin.

To this day, she recognizes the disease for what it is and holds her family responsible for their abuse. One day at a time, she does not act out with men and is currently engaged to be married to a kind, respectful man who has joined her on the journey of recovery. Lillian is recovering her innate sense of self and her internal ability to care for herself.

We believe this *innate sense** of self-care and self-love is given to each person by the Divine at birth. This innate sense of self-care and self-empowerment is a great gift. Whenever we are involved in or victimized by an addictive/dysfunctional system such as our family of origin, church, or educational environments, our innate sense of self is diminished or completely unavailable for our access.

The tapes of our childhood abuse play over and over again, telling us we deserve this abuse, something is wrong with us, and so on. These messages of childhood abuse are internalized. The tapes play even after we stop hearing them from our offenders. We replay them over and over again. It is all we know, and it becomes a part of our identity. When there is intervention concerning our disease, our "victim thinking" must be exposed in order to begin to change our own "victim behavior." This is the most painful part of the recovery process. Often these tapes and messages of shame and unworthiness have gone on inside of us without conscious awareness. When this awareness becomes conscious, the tapes and messages are exposed.

Often, this is a time when people want to leave or actually stop their recovery. The uncovering of these painful thoughts and the internalized shame that we have carried from our abusers, behaviors, and internalized beliefs are often too painful to embrace. However, this is a necessary part of our recovery. If we are able to weather this painful part of our recovery, continued healing and growth will take place. When intervention in our thoughts, bodies, and spirits occurs, it is brought out into the open, and recovery begins and deepens over time.

Another less dramatic example of how co-sex addicts carry the shame of their abusers is clearly distinguished in Jennifer's recovery.

JENNIFER'S STORY

When Jennifer was growing up with her four brothers and father, they consistently commented on women's looks, particularly breast size and body weight. The men in her family sexualized interactions with women regularly in front of Jennifer. When she reached adolescence, they commented on her body changes and physical development. They laughed and acted shamelessly when commenting on her femininity and what she could "do for a man." Jennifer carried their shame and consistently felt shameful about her own growth and development as a woman. The sacred and wonderful time of her transition into womanhood was not embraced and encouraged as such, but became a time of fear and shame.

As Jennifer entered high school, she became less and less interested in learning and excelling academically. She began to internalize the dysfunctional belief of her father that her only value was in her body and attractiveness. She had been trained by her family of origin that her value resided in her looks and her body and breast size, so she focused all her energy and attention on getting this approval from her male peers and keeping herself "looking good." She was so obsessed with her looks that she missed out on experiencing and developing her natural athletic ability and aptitude for learning.

She married a sex addict who overfocused on her looks and used her sexually whenever he needed a fix. Socially, she was a "trophy" on his arm. As she began to age and mature, she began to internally panic that her looks were fading and she could not keep her husband interested. Because all of her value was in her looks, when her looks changed, her value began to diminish. She felt such shame and fear that she had breast implants and put herself through many surgical procedures to try to enhance her beauty.

When she discovered her husband was addicted to Internet pornography, this increased her feeling of shame that she was not enough, pretty enough, or sexy enough, and that if she were, he would not be acting out.

As she entered recovery, she was able to uncover the deeply held beliefs she carried from her brothers and father that a woman's value was in her looks and sexuality. She also uncovered the dysfunctional belief that a woman's value also came from how she could please a man. Jennifer confronted her brothers about how they had sexualized her and women in general and did not tolerate their comments any longer. In therapy, she was able to work out these same issues with her father, who had died years before.

Jennifer began to grieve her losses around these beliefs and develop healthful boundaries around her husband and other men in her life. She confronted her husband's sex addiction and no longer took responsibility for his behavior nor carried his shame.

She no longer saw her worth as related only to her looks and no longer carried the shame of their shameless beliefs and behaviors.

She went back to school to fulfill a lifelong dream of pursuing a higher education. As she began to value her intellect, spirit, creativity, and all aspects of being a woman, she and her husband's relationship deepened, and they began to experience genuine closeness and intimacy.

Jennifer's story is an example of how one confronts shame and reclaims self-empowerment. In therapy, Jennifer was able to begin her family of origin work, which began with coming out of denial, confronting the abuse and abusers, and learning how to take care of and nurture herself. At the same time, Jennifer was actively involved in a co-sex addiction recovery program. In using the tools of the program, she got a sponsor, attended regular 12-step meetings, and began her written step work.

To begin to make the transition between shame and empowerment, co-sex addicts must begin by acknowledging the Co-Sex Addicts Anonymous's first step: we admitted we were powerless over co-sex addiction and others' sex addiction and that our lives had become unmanageable.

Once we are able to acknowledge powerlessness over our own and another's disease, we begin to lose the shame we've carried for our abusers and the disease. This is also an ability that has been lost to us that we now reclaim. This is the ability to experience "healthy anger." With healthy anger, we are able to experience when we are being abused, used, and not fully respected and honored for who we are. Healthy anger allows us the wisdom and strength to consistently confront abusers who consciously or unconsciously attempt to use us to carry their shame. With our anger, we can choose boundaries, energetically and physically, that keep us from "taking on" negative effects of someone else's behavior.

EXAMPLE: Jean recalls an incident when she, her husband, and her three adult children were at family therapy. During the initial session, the counselor confronted Michael, Jean's husband, for his verbally abusive behavior. Rather than owning this behavior, Michael became defensive and enraged, but did so silently.

At the therapy break, he raged about the counselor to Jean, who immediately "took on" his feelings of shame, which he was not acknowledging. Still on the break, Jean stormed back and confronted the therapist while Michael just walked away smiling. Jean and Michael's adult children witnessed this exchange.

When the counseling session resumed and the family was together, the adult children confronted their parents about this exchange. They helped Jean and Michael see that this was a common dynamic in their family: Dad raged, and Mom carried the shame and acted it out.

After Jean understood her part of this dynamic, she began to use her healthy anger to set a boundary in her relationship with Michael, and she stopped carrying and acting out his shame and his other feelings. Michael was then able to begin to deal honestly with his own feelings and learn healthy self-care and good boundaries as well.

This is an especially challenging aspect of co-sex addiction recovery for women. In our society, women begin to be conditioned as little girls to be "nice," "take care of others," and "be available for men." Women are conditioned to be valued for their looks and physical appearance rather than their inner strength, brilliant thinking, and highly intuitive abilities. For a woman to begin to reclaim her innate ability to care for herself and also to claim her healthy anger, she must confront the internal messages that tell her she must be nice or that "nice girls don't get angry," as well as the societal messages that tell her the same and that her value is in how she looks and "takes care of her man."

As we begin our path of recovery, it is essential to look at how shame has been in our lives and understand how important it is to connect this shame that we carry with those who abused us. We rid ourselves of this shame by confronting our own disease and our abusers and returning their shame to them. We believe this must occur early in our recovery or the shame will keep us from doing the necessary work for healing from our disease.

SHAME AS AN
INTERGENERATIONAL DISEASE

Another way that shame adds fuel to our disease and creates an intergenerational "shame connection" is when we shame others. Oftentimes, it is our children. When we do not acknowledge and work directly on shame, we act in a variety of ways to try to rid ourselves of this horrible feeling.

Once again, we wish to distinguish shame and guilt. We believe there is "healthy" guilt in which we hold ourselves accountable and our children and/or others accountable for their behavior. Healthy guilt teaches us that we have somehow contradicted our own value system. In this way, guilt is a gift. Shame differs from guilt in that it tells us we are "bad" or "wrong," not that we *made* a mistake but that we *are* a mistake. When we do not work on our carried shame, we pass it on to others.

When we shame others, we pass the intergenerational shame on. They walk away feeling shame—that they are bad, wrong, or worthless—while we may have a "momentary" release from the feeling of shame because we just acted on it by doing a "shame dump" on someone else. This momentary release is similar to the addictive cycle of the building of tension and then getting a momentary fix that releases the tension. The addictive release is temporary and only adds to the shame we are already carrying and have passed on to a new generation, as is the case with our children. Of course, the victims of our shame "dump" may be others: friends, spouse, strangers, and so on. Not only that, but those we shamed now carry this shame and must find other victims for temporary dumping of the shame they now carry. We see from this example how powerful, intergenerational, and strong this disease is. Without recovery intervention, this disease will progress and continue in this cycle.

Remember, we distinguished shame as "what happens to us" and guilt as "what we have done." The shame we carried belongs to someone else who is unwilling or unable to experience his own healthy remorse, and we take it in as shame and something wrong about us. Guilt is what reminds us that we need to take responsibility for our own behavior, have contradicted our own healthy value system, and may need to alter our behaviors and make amends.

Once we take this huge step of embracing the shame and returning it to our abusers, we can begin to reclaim our innate sense of self. Our healthy anger is necessary in order to do this. Equally as difficult is owning our own abusive behavior and beginning to take responsibility for our "shaming" of others. Within the co-sex addict and sex addict dynamic, the sex addict is the Big Offender using others to carry his shame. The co-sex addict is the Big Victim and the little offender because her primary role is victim. She carries the shame for the sex addict and then acts it out with her little offender on others.

Co-sex addiction and shame create a compulsive, obsessive, and multifaceted disease. It can be acted out in many different forms of dysfunctional behavior. This dysfunctional behavior can be acted out in our relationships with others other than our partner. This behavior can also be acted out on ourselves when we internalize the shame of our family of origin or another individual.

Some ways we act out the internalized shame in addition to our COSA behaviors include overeating, compulsive shopping, bingeing, alcohol and drug abuse, raging, and so on.

EXAMPLE: Sandra was visiting her family recently. During the meal, someone commented on how lovely she was, and her verbally abusive aunt said, "Yes, she has always been pretty, but now she is getting old." Sandra, unable to confront her aunt's shaming, internalized the comment and began to overeat. Later, Sandra realized her behavior and was able to feel her feelings about the incident. Having

done much family of origin work, Sandra was able to see how her
aunt's verbally abusive COSA behavior was just another way of acting
out the shame she carried from her sex addict husband. Sandra's aunt
had been married to an alcoholic man who had many affairs and was
both physically and verbally abusive to her. She carried his shame,
internalized it, and acted it out with others in her life.

Sandra was also able to recall her direct experience with this uncle, whom
she always felt uneasy around. During her preadolescence, she also recalls his
touching her breasts in a "teasing way"; however, she now knows that he was
acting out his sexual addiction with her directly. This is an example of the
multigenerational impact sex addiction and co-sex addiction has on a family
and how the shame is acted out by both the co-sex addict and the sex addict.
This is diagrammed in the figure below.

Figure 4. Intergenerational Shaming

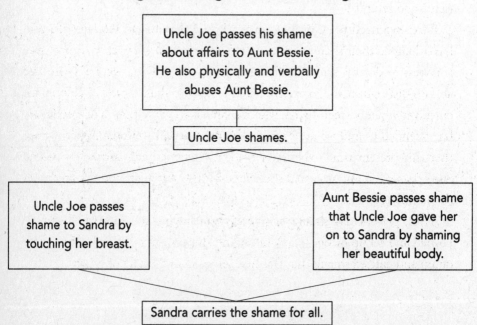

Uncle Joe passes his shame about affairs to Aunt Bessie. He also physically and verbally abuses Aunt Bessie.

Uncle Joe shames.

Uncle Joe passes shame to Sandra by touching her breast.

Aunt Bessie passes shame that Uncle Joe gave her on to Sandra by shaming her beautiful body.

Sandra carries the shame for all.

SHAME REDUCTION WORK AND RAGE

As co-sex addicts, we must do *shame reduction** and *healing work.** One of the most important tools we learn in recovery from co-sex addiction is the awareness of our feeling of shame and the ability to distinguish the carried shame we have from those who've offended us. If we think of healthy shame as energy as light as a butterfly, this will help us. We have just enough shame to know to put clothes on before we go outside and to know we are not the Divine or as perfect as God.

The process of reducing shame is to look at incidents when others put their unhealthy shame on us. For a child, this shaming comes from those in authority, generally adults such as a teacher, minister, priest, relatives, or parents. For adult women, this would be anyone we view as authority, including our partners, priests, supervisors, and so on.

This *shame dump** occurs during any form of abuse that is not accompanied by amends or healthy remorse. Without getting rid of our carried shame, authentic relationships cannot occur. Shame is a block to intimacy, authenticity, and serenity.

Often we need to confront people whose behavior has offended us, who have dumped their shame on us, and whose shame we now carry. Sometimes it is best to do this symbolically, not face-to-face. When we are aware and able to distinguish the experience and feeling of shame, we are able to ask ourselves when we feel shame, whose shame is it? More than likely, someone has offended us and we are carrying their shame. As we look deeper, we see that this present-time experience of being offended and carrying someone else's shame has also triggered the shame we are carrying that originated from our family of origin.

Thus, present-day shame originates from having our internal "buttons" pushed and set up by our family of origin. This button is set up by the shame dump and carried shame that was first set up in our family of origin.

EXAMPLE: Amy was no longer in a relationship with her first boss. He was very shaming, cursing her and telling her that she was stupid on a regular basis. Her father had often said the same thing when she was a child, and so each time her boss shamed her as an adult, it was as though her dad had stepped into the room. Her original hurt was re-created, so it felt like a double dose of shame—one from her boss and the other triggered from her father. In therapy, Amy was able to confront her father for the original shame dump and do some shame reduction work. She used her healthy anger to symbolically confront her father for setting her up to be shamed by her boss. Once she did this original shame reduction work with her father, she was able to confront her boss in abusive situations.

This is a good time to talk about rage. Rage distinguished from healthy anger is necessary. We define rage as the combined feelings of anger and shame. When these feelings of pent-up anger and shame come together, the result is rage. Rage is abusive and not part of healthy recovery. The rage cycle also perpetuates shame being passed on from person to person, and shame is the fuel of addiction.

In recovery, as our awareness of the shame that we carry increases, we can intervene on our own internal or external shaming behaviors. Then we are left with the feeling of healthy anger, which is a guide for aiding us in protecting ourselves. We learn to use our anger as strength to set boundaries, confront offensive behavior, and take other necessary actions for self-care and self-protection in our recovery. We believe that healthy anger is necessary in order for us to take action in setting boundaries and to stop carrying the shame of others.

The following is another example of intervening on the shame cycle and doing shame reduction work.

EXAMPLE: After many years in recovery, Lilli had learned how to recognize someone else's offensive behavior and when she was feeling shame around it. One visit with her older brother brought this home to her. At a family gathering, he snapped an insult at her, insinuating she was stupid. In her past, she would have felt shame about herself, believing she was stupid, and becoming meek and quiet around her family. In this incident, however, she immediately felt some healthy anger with her brother's behavior and confronted him. Even though she had a moment of "taking on his shame," she was able to recognize this old pattern, confront and hold him accountable for his insulting and offensive behavior, and not take in the shame as being about her.

This new behavior of confronting her brother on the spot had come after years of family of origin work that included reading incidents in a group setting, 12-step recovery work with a sponsor, and attending 12-step co-sex addict meetings. She also had many opportunities to practice confronting people's offensive and inappropriate behavior that were less challenging than the original abuse with her brother.

Changing this victim/offender dynamic of carrying shame takes great intention and consistent work. The behavior was learned young as a survival tactic, so intervention on many levels was necessary. Lilli did shame reduction work in therapy, with her sponsor, and in various workshops. She took many risks in confronting people and behaving differently. Talking about these challenges and changes in therapy and her 12-step meetings gave her a lot of support and encouragement to confront her shaming offenders, set boundaries, and care for herself in these relationships.

Once shame intervention occurs, we begin to develop healthy boundaries with a strong refusal to continue to be victimized by carrying the shame of our abusers and acting it out. If the relationship of the co-sex addict and sex addict is to grow and deepen in genuine intimacy, the sex addict must begin to take responsibility for this shame dumping, and the co-sex addict must be willing to take responsibility for carrying this shame and acting it out. When both partners are able to own their Big Offender and Big Victim and then little victim and little offender, true healing can begin.

With this new awareness of ourselves as strong, valuable women, we also reclaim our ability to care for ourselves and nurture our own divine purposes and callings in the world. Once we have intervened on the carried shame that we have held for so long, and done the shame reduction and healing work, we begin to have a restored sense of self. Our intuition and innate sense of self-care become apparent to us.

Our recovery becomes visible in our lives. Our well-being in all areas increases, including our physical and spiritual health, and authentic intimacy in our relationships with ourselves and others will emerge.

The innate sense of self-care and self-love that our addictions and the carried shame have taken from us begin to return as we deal with the issues of our co-sex addict disease. The following signs indicate that we are regaining our innate sense of self-care and self-love:

1. We have the innate sense that we are separate from the Divine; we are not God.

2. We have the innate sense to know how to set boundaries with others, to say no and to say yes when appropriate.

3. This innate sense reminds us that we are separate from others and not responsible for anyone else's behavior but our own.

4. We are given the innate sense of modesty and self-expression in ways that respect ourselves and others.

5. While we have the innate sense of our separateness from a Higher Power, we also have the innate sense of our intimate connection with the Divine and the expansive nature of our own personal power.

6. Our vitality and energy may increase.

7. We experience a sense of lightness, and our outward appearance may become softer.

8. Our inner beauty begins to be visible outwardly.

9. We begin to distinguish between carried shame and healthy guilt, as well as take responsibility when we hurt ourselves or others. We make amends for our behavior.

10. Amends for our behavior, when we discover we have contradicted our own value system, will deepen our healthy and authentic connection to ourselves and others.

11. We begin to love ourselves, acknowledging our unique gifts and developing compassion for our own imperfections.

12. Our relationships are more fulfilling and authentic, and we consistently choose to be in connection with others who demonstrate respect, maturity, and healthy emotional availability.

This innate sense of self-care and self-empowerment is a great gift. Whenever we are involved with or victimized by an addictive/dysfunctional system such as our family of origin, society, church, or educational environments, our innate sense of self is diminished by the shame. Reclaiming this great gift restores our authentic connection to ourselves, our Higher Power, and to others.

5

Trusting and Embracing Feelings

*T*he 12-step work of Co-Sex Addicts Anonymous (based on the 12 steps of Alcoholics Anonymous) is where we can begin to embrace and learn to trust our feelings, using our emotions to guide us through the healing and recovery in our lives.

There is no real recovery without reclaiming our ability to feel and embrace our feelings. And, of course, herein lies the challenge. The reason that we became co-sex addicts and began acting out these obsessive/compulsive behaviors was to *avoid* our feelings and put our attention on anything but the pain we carried within our bodies.

An addictive/dysfunctional system, within which we were set up as addicts, has two fundamental dynamics: (1) We are wounded (physically, sexually, emotionally, intellectually, spiritually, or any combination), and once this wounding occurs, we take on the shame and make the abuse about us; and, (2) We then deny the ability to feel our pain (feelings) or talk about what happened with honesty and emotional presence.

Eventually, after multiple woundings, we learn to survive by stuffing our feelings, shutting down our emotions, denying that anything is wrong, and/or by using any number of survival behaviors that we take on for protection.

Human beings are born with an innate ability, need, and desire for self-expression of their feelings. When hurt, a child will naturally cry to release sadness. There are other times a child will naturally express anger to assert their self-care and express fear when they sense they are in unsafe situations, which is also part of self-care.

When the dysfunctional/addictive family wounds the child and causes her/his feelings to *shut down*,* the child learns to deny her/his feeling self and even loses the ability to feel emotions such as joy.

> **EXAMPLE:** Vanessa recalls her elementary education experiences. She was a high achiever and often earned academic and athletic awards during her early years in school. As a recovering co-sex addict, she is able to recall never feeling joy, pride, or accomplishment with any of these achievements. Vanessa felt either shame or nothing at all. She also recalls the sense of "it's not enough," and this drove her to continue achieving. She realizes now that she was unable to feel joy, and her compulsive/addictive behavior to try to fill the emptiness and shame inside resulted in constant overachieving.
>
> Vanessa's sister, Joan, is also in recovery. She is able to recall her role in the dysfunctional family system as well. Whatever Joan accomplished, she was compared to her "hero" sister, so her accomplishments were also "never enough." Since she received no attention at all for her accomplishments, Joan learned to not try to fill the emptiness with achievement, but soon began acting out her emptiness by getting into trouble and underachieving.

Again, the greatest challenge, as well as the greatest joy, of co-sex addiction recovery is the "reclaiming" and "embracing" of our emotions.

For simplicity, we acknowledge six basic feelings. They are: *sadness*, *anger*, *fear*, *guilt*, *shame*, and *joy*. When wounded as children, whether intentionally or unintentionally, by someone in our family of origin or by anyone in an authority role, we may experience one or any combination of the above emotions. If we are in a safe environment where we are not subject to repeated and chronic wounding, and where our feelings are listened to and acknowledged, we are able to express these emotions and naturally heal from the wound. If we are denied the ability to express our feelings repeatedly, as is the case in addictive/dysfunctional systems, we will seek compulsive or obsessive ways to cope with these repeated hurts. This is the source of the disease and of our addictions that we carry into adulthood.

With intervention and recovery, we begin to truly feel our feelings and find supportive and safe environments to express them. Over time, we can slowly begin to notice how we are feeling in the moment rather than continuing to act out these emotions in addictive ways. We believe the most powerful context for this recovery is in co-sex addiction 12-step recovery.

EXAMPLE: Annie recalls a couple of years into her co-sex addiction recovery how clearly her addictive behavior was related to not feeling certain emotions.

She was beginning to come out of denial about the behaviors she used, including her substance addiction to food, to alter her feelings. In her therapy group, she shared with the group how she had just been introduced to a man that she found very attractive and who immediately fit her ideal of a "good husband." After their first meeting, she found herself thinking of this man almost constantly. She imagined what her first name sounded like with his last name and pictured the children and family they would have together. When she shared this in her therapy group, she received agreement that this was one of her "mood-altering" behaviors similar to drinking for an alcoholic and compulsively eating, as she had done as well. Her therapist suggested that she spend the next week gently pinching herself on the arm as a reminder any time she was fantasizing or futurizing about someone or something other than being present in the moment. She was to tell herself where she was, what day it was, and what she was doing.

When Annie arrived in therapy the following week, she shared how stunned she was to learn how many minutes in the day she spent thinking about something outside of the very moment she was living in. She shared with her group and the therapist how she found herself pinching her arm to get her back into the moment she was in. This, combined with her recovery from compulsive overeating, helped her more and more to stay in her body and feel her own feelings in the moment. Annie learned a great deal about the various behaviors she used to not feel what was going on with her in the moment.

Once in recovery, these women began to own and acknowledge their feelings. They also did their family of origin work, and in safe environments they were able to grieve and release their emotions from their past as well.

Another important step in recovery is trusting our feelings and allowing them to guide our actions. As women in co-sex addiction recovery, we learn to appreciate our feelings as powerful guides that help us take care of ourselves responsibly. We learn to trust each feeling we experience as having an important gift for us in self-care.

SADNESS

Sadness gives us the gift of healing. When we can authentically feel and express our sadness over our own hurt or past abuses, as well as sadness over the powerlessness we have over this disease, we are able to stay in reality. This ability to feel the loss associated with how we were hurt is essential to recovery.

When we feel our sadness and allow our tears, healing immediately follows. Feeling our grief keeps us present in our *authentic reality*.* It also allows us to stay connected to our Higher Power and helps us know what we can do and what we must surrender. This is the gift of healing that sadness provides when we are willing to embrace our losses and grief. On the other hand, when healthy sadness is combined with shame and we are unable to distinguish between them, the sadness can become overwhelming *depression*.*

ANGER

Anger's gift is strength to make boundaries and to take action for self-care. Anger is about knowing how and when to protect ourselves. It also guides us in staying in reality and teaches us how to choose respectful, healthy people as models, partners, and friends.

Anger is a natural, healthy response to being offended. As childhood victims of abuse, however, we do not learn how to have healthy anger to protect ourselves. We do not know how to stand up for ourselves with boundaries, nor do we have strong, healthy adults to go to when we are hurt or abused. Therefore, learning to have healthy anger and to use the strength of that anger to set boundaries becomes a vital aspect of co-sex addiction recovery. On the other hand, when healthy anger is combined with shame, it can become debilitating rage.

FEAR

Fear's gift gives us the knowledge and wisdom to protect ourselves. In our family of origin, we learned early on to shut down the feeling of fear as a way to survive. Often in the early stages of our recovery, when we have begun to thaw all those frozen feelings inside, we may confuse those feelings from our herstories with feelings in present time.

After some family of origin work and time in recovery, the wisdom that comes with fear assists us in distinguishing our history from what is happening today. That stuffed fear has become terror, and we learn to use the steps of recovery to embrace our powerfulness over our histories. We also grieve our past and use the wisdom of fear to guide us in our current relationships.

Here is where the assistance of a good sponsor, meetings, and therapy help us make the distinctions. With our support system, we have help in separating fear from terror. We believe terror is an "overblown" feeling of fear based in our childhood. As children, our survival required us to stuff all of our feelings of fear, and this feeling of fear became terror. For a child, who is helpless, this becomes overwhelming.

In recovery, we learn to recognize our inner voice that tells us "something is wrong." When we place that old fear and terror in our own herstories, we can then use our healthy fear to guide us in present time. We begin to respect that feeling of fear so we are able to protect ourselves rather than live in terror or feel terrorized. There is great wisdom in the feeling of fear, but when fear is combined with shame, we experience debilitating terror.

GUILT

Guilt's gift to us is the ability to know our values. In recovery we learn about ourselves, our own integrity, what we value, and what is important to us. Therefore, when we contradict our own values, we experience healthy guilt as a reminder.

As children, we are shamed and hurt so often, we do not know the difference between shame and guilt. The healthy emotional, intellectual, and spiritual development of our own values is interrupted in the dysfunctional and addictive system. Children in this system do not have an opportunity to integrate and learn their own values. They are primarily in survival mode and carrying the shame of the offenders in the family.

In recovery, we learn what our values are in our own lives. We learn to "give back" the shame that we carry from those who abused us, and we learn to distinguish guilt from shame. Healthy guilt teaches us when we have violated our values by our own behavior either by hurting ourselves or another person. *It would be helpful here to remember that shame is something done to us, while guilt is about our own actions and what we have done.*

SHAME

Shame's gift is humility. We are given just enough to know we are not God and to put clothes on when we go outside. Any more than that is an indication of what has happened to us and the carried shame that we still carry for our offenders. When we feel this carried shame, we are reminded of a boundary we may need to set. It might also be an indication of an old wound in our herstories and some work that still needs to be accomplished.

JOY

Joy's gift is fulfillment and connection. When we allow ourselves to do the grief work concerning our pain, carried shame, fear, anger, and guilt, we open ourselves for perhaps the greatest gift of doing our feeling work: experiencing joy. Embracing our authentic joy and sharing it with others creates connection. It is also our belief that this creates fulfillment from within. It creates a connection with our Higher Power and opens up the path to gratitude.

In dysfunctional families, even joy is often not an allowed feeling. Many co-sex addicts share that it is within their co-sex addiction recovery that they first begin to experience the emotions of joy, gratitude, and authentic connection.

Even though we realize that it is our pent-up feelings and pain that we had been avoiding in our disease, we now realize our feelings are our greatest gift. We also know that to the extent that we allow ourselves to feel our pain and grief is the extent to which we allow ourselves to feel our joy as well.

6

Body Image and Dysfunctional Eating Versus Healthy Self-Care

This disease is very powerful and extends throughout all areas of our lives. Most co-sex addicts have a distorted body image and some degree of an eating disorder. When a woman feels her only value is in whether or not she is loved by a man or in a relationship with a man, an inordinate amount of energy is focused on how to secure this relationship. In our society, one of the ways co-sex addiction is enabled is the overfocus on appearance, especially for women.

Older men who appear in ads look distinguished and powerful. It is rare that older women appear in ads at all. Most ads of women are of very thin, young girls/women. The most common are all the same size and shape, often enhanced with surgery for looks and appeal to the men in our society.

When a little girl is not encouraged to develop her mind, talents, and emotional and spiritual potential, and primarily taught to focus on physical appearance, much is lost. This is a loss for both men and women. We become brainwashed by what our culture says is important. The richness of a woman's thinking, creativity, wisdom, intuition, and intellect all take a backseat to her appearance, and since youth is part of the equation of looking good, there is even more dismissed about the whole value of a woman as she ages. In growing up with emotional, sexual and/or *physical abuse** and neglect, she will eventually begin to shut down her feeling self, which produces a breeding ground for obsessive/compulsive disorders. Her focus becomes on how she can look good for a man. Physical appearance becomes a constant thought. Again, it is something on the outside that is falsely believed to fulfill the emptiness on the inside.

Marianne's Story

I remember being a very lonely and sad child. My father died when I was young, and I often felt starved for attention. I turned to food. This was also a setup for co-sex addiction. It was one of the few moments in which my attention was turned from the emptiness inside to something outside of myself. Eating was a temporary respite from the emotional numbness inside.

By high school, I was obsessed with being thin and with never being quite thin or pretty enough. Even if I felt good and had a temporary "high" from losing weight, it was short-lived, and there was always some new or old imperfection in my body that became my focus. During my sophomore year in college, my roommates taught me this great new way to stay thin, and we all began on a regular basis to "throw up" our food. I was very excited with this great new tool for finally being thin. I became an active bulimic and would vow to throw up "just this one more time" and then never do it again. This went on for almost seven years until I finally sought help with a professional therapist and then Overeaters Anonymous. At first, the therapist wanted to talk about my family and my feelings. One day, feeling exasperated, I said to her, "I don't want to talk about my feelings or family. I just want you to tell me how to stop throwing up my food!" Her reply was, "Learn to tolerate your feelings."

Needless to say, I had no idea what she meant, but I continued with professional counseling and my own 12-step work. Things began to sink in, and I began to be able to identify my feelings. I could communicate them to others and actually began to learn boundaries and good self-care. One day I was having a conversation with an old friend, and she made a very indirect and unkind remark. I asked her to explain what she meant by it and to clarify if I had done something to upset her. She began to yell and accuse me of all sorts of things. I could not get a word in edgewise, and eventually she hung up the phone in a rage. I was shocked. The next thing I remember is standing in front of the open refrigerator door, frantically scanning up and down the shelves for something to eat. I don't recall exactly how long I stood there, but suddenly I heard myself say, "I'm not hungry. I'm angry!" At that moment, I slammed the door and sat down to let it all sink in.

This was a breakthrough in my recovery, eating disorder, and co-sex addiction. I made the connection between "tolerating my feelings" and "acting them out." I realized that for years I could not identify my feelings. I used food to medicate myself and stuff my feelings down, especially when I was angry. I did not believe I even had a right to be angry. I had learned to shut down emotionally and then become obsessed with my body image, food, and being just a little thinner. This was safer than feeling, but no more. It was an insightful moment for me and a turning point in my healing.

It is in the midst of this culture and dysfunctional thinking about the value of women that eating disorders, distorted body images, and obsessive/compulsive behaviors concerning eating, exercise, and physical appearance begin and grow.

When sexual abuse occurs, often a cycle of overeating begins as well. This may be a conscious or unconscious way the victim attempts to hide herself and her body and hopefully disappear from the sex abuser's radar. Her family may also try to cover up the abuse by covering up the victim. Encouraging her to be overweight and hiding her sexuality can be an attempt to hide from the outside world the sexual abuse that has taken place in the past or may currently be happening. This is a setup for the little girl to grow into adulthood with an eating disorder, distorted body image, sexual dysfunction, and more.

There is another side to the way in which sexual abuse sets a girl up as a woman with eating/body issues. If a little girl is sexualized, either with direct sexual abuse or through the emotional dynamic of the family, she may grow into adolescence and adulthood believing that her only value is her sexuality. She may dress very provocatively throughout adolescence, develop bulimic/anorexic tendencies, and keep herself very thin and looking "sexy" for boys/men. These girls may grow into women who have plastic surgery repeatedly, wear short skirts and high heels, and oftentimes deprive themselves of a balance of healthy nutrition and physical activity.

Eating disorders and dysfunctional body image behaviors that have developed from sexual abuse may include the following:

- Starving oneself
- Bulimia (bingeing and purging with food by compulsive exercise after eating, throwing up food after eating, using herbal or synthetic laxatives, fasting, compulsive dieting, etc.)
- Dressing to expose the body in inappropriately short skirts, tight shirts, and so on, or alternately dressing in baggy clothes or clothes that hide the body
- Overeating and using food to medicate feelings
- Overfocusing on body "perfection" and losing the ability to be in reality about how we really look

- Getting breast implants and/or other invasive surgeries to attempt to live up to society's definition and indoctrination of "beauty."

- Keeping on excess weight to avoid experiencing that we are sexual beings and to avoid dealing with any sexual abuse of our past

- Being excessively thin to avoid experiencing that we are sexual beings and to avoid dealing with any sexual abuse of our past

In our opinion and experience, there is an extremely high correlation between sexual abuse and eating disorders. Quite often, women must first deal with their substance addiction (food, alcohol, drugs, etc.) prior to getting in touch with the original abuse that set them up as co-sex addicts.

7

Addiction/Money Dysfunction Versus Abundance

*S*ince the core of co-sex addiction is based in the setup of being a victim, this often transfers to the financial arena of a co-sex addict's life and/or in her partnership. Oftentimes, being a victim translates into a woman being unable or unwilling to be financially independent through her own contributions. This gets set up in the family through a lack of education about financial matters and the spoken or unspoken belief that all the woman needs to do is look good so she can find herself a man to take care of her financially. This occurs in society as well, through institutions that impart a belief of feminine submission and/or dependency for women. It is not often that women are empowered to be bold, strong, and independent leaders.

Many times, in a partnership, the co-sex addict is financially dependent on the addict and does not have an empowered role in managing the money, knowing how it is being spent, or how it is distributed. Since looking good is often characteristic of the addictive system, the addict may be "generously" providing for the co-sex addict and "gifting" for both necessities and luxuries. Here, the addict is still in control of how the money is spent and distributed, while the co-sex addict has no voice or knowledge about the details of income and expenses.

Another highly common and dysfunctional example of the addict's/co-addict's behavior around money is in the arena of gift giving. There is often an unspoken agreement between the sex addict and the co-sex addict that luxury gifts such as jewelry or furs are given with strings attached. This string often comes in the form of sex. When a sex addict gives a gift, the co-sex addict is expected to perform sexually as a thank-you for this exchange. This is clearly another form of manipulation, control, and enabling that is characteristic of the dysfunction of a co-sex addict and her sex addict partner.

Money is the form of exchange of goods and services within our culture. It can often be misused as a form of manipulation and/or control. It is our belief that a co-sex addict must find her voice and personal power within the financial arena in her own life and most especially within the life of her partnership with her sex addict.

Gifts are often confused with love by the sex addict and co-sex addict. He may lavish material things on her in order to make up for his absence or acting out in or outside of the relationship. She wonders why she feels abandoned when he is showering her with diamonds, clothes, and so on. All she may want is his time, commitment, and attention to the relationship. Gifts are spoiled by the emotional and physical abandonment of the partner. The co-sex addict is left angry and manipulated, with a sense of craziness, as everyone thinks "he is so great" as he lavishes her with material things. Because our society places great value on material things, this internal sense of craziness that the co-sex addict carries is reinforced outside of the partnership as well. Because the material gifts do not come from a place of authentic relationship and connection, they are simply another form of manipulation and abuse, keeping in place the addictive cycle.

EXAMPLE: Warren was a financially successful businessman and was in the habit of providing very nice "gifts" to Jeannine, his wife. Warren "gifted" Jeannine a station wagon for Christmas. His car is a luxury car that is considered a business necessity. On the surface,

Warren looks like a generous giver, but further scrutiny reveals otherwise.

First of all, Jeannine needs an automobile for carpooling, taxiing children, and regular household responsibilities, such as grocery shopping, doctors' appointments, and so on. Providing transportation for the family is the responsibility of the adults. Warren appears generous in his giving, but in truth, Jeannine has a right to choose her own automobile. She should have the right to determine her own needs and wants concerning this item. She also has a right and a financial responsibility to know what expenses Warren is incurring in his large and small purchases. She has a right to have a voice in determining financial expenditures.

We also have experience with women who financially bankrupted themselves for the approval and "love" of a sex addict. There are also countless stories of a sex addict acting outside of the marriage and spending thousands of dollars in his addiction.

$\mathscr{L}$ORRENA'S $\mathscr{S}$TORY

Don failed to pay Social Security taxes one year, and Ruth, Don's ex-wife, claimed the kids as deductions one year, leaving Don owing about $5,000 to $7,000. I found this out after we were married a month or two. He had been ignoring the IRS, which resulted in high penalties and interest. I told him that we had to start paying this off.

Don had two defaulted student loans totaling more than $20,000 due to penalties and interest. Again, I found this out within a month or two of getting married and asked him to start making payments.

Don had a warrant out for his arrest for an unpaid traffic ticket. This really scared me, but he was very nonchalant about it. I found this out within about six months of being married.

Don's parents gave him $20,000 to pay off his student loan. Instead, he decided that he wanted to buy a new house and use that money for a down payment, flooring, decorating, furniture, and so on. About a week after moving in, I found out that Don was a sex addict and that he had spent a lot of the money acting out. We ended up in debt for all of the flooring, were unable to do any decorating, had very little furniture in most rooms, and had two empty rooms because we couldn't buy any furniture. We had ordered some furniture direct from South Carolina that arrived a few days after we moved in. Since he had spent the money, we ended up with more than $5,000 additional debt and had to make monthly payments. He was having an affair with a topless dancer and bought her a $500 computer for Christmas on credit. We had to make those monthly payments for about a year, as he had also purchased the same computer for his kids.

Eight months later, I found out that Don was still acting out, and I told him that he had to go to residential treatment or leave the house. He decided to go to treatment for twenty-eight days, which cost us $28,000. We were required to put about $6,000 down, so we had to use a credit card. After a long battle with the insurance company, they agreed to pay for six days of treatment, totaling $6,000. They let us pay out the remaining $18,000, so we were making monthly payments to the center and to the credit card company for his treatment.

A year and a half later, we were getting back approximately $4,000 to $5,000 from the IRS, and we were going to apply it all to debt. A furniture truck pulled up on our street one day and went door-to-door asking if people wanted to buy any furniture. They supplied all of the model homes in the subdivision, and when the builders didn't use all of the pieces, they sold the extra furniture in the neighborhoods. Don checked out the company and made sure their story was reputable. He went out in a heavy rain to see the furniture and got all excited that we could finish furnishing our house with the dining room set and living room furniture without going into debt by using our income tax money. I was always embarrassed that our home looked so bare and felt that all of our money went toward paying for his old debt and his addiction. I agreed to use the income tax money for the furniture.

A couple of years down the road, Don became obsessed with looking for a table and chairs for our breakfast room. We had been using a very ugly table and chairs from his bachelor days that I thought were so horrible. I told him that I didn't want any more monthly payments. He started e-mailing and calling me several times a day asking me to go online and look at pictures of various pieces of furniture that he liked. I think he spent most of his days at work searching for exactly what he wanted. I kept telling him no. Finally, he asked me to just go look at the breakfast set with him, along with some living room tables that he liked. I resisted for quite some time and eventually agreed to look. I saw a few sets that were very inexpensive but plain, and I thought maybe we could get something like that without going into debt. Don asked me to just look at what he had picked out, and when I did, I agreed that it was very beautiful. Then he showed me the living room tables he liked, which were also very beautiful. He asked me to fill out a credit application just to see how much our monthly payments would be. The furniture cost about $2,000, but if we purchased $2,500 of furniture, we could get financing for one year with no interest. So we picked out a table to put our TV on and the cost was now $2,500. I started thinking about how nice it would be to get rid of the ugly breakfast room furniture and finish furnishing the living area. Don knew that if he could just get me to look at something, I might be more likely to agree to purchase it, and we did.

Four years ago, Hanah, Don's daughter, made a suicide attempt and was placed in a hospital. Several months later, she had to return, and we had to find a wilderness program for her, followed by residential treatment. We made payments to the hospital and had to put several thousand dollars on a credit card because we didn't know how else we would be able to pay for her care. The wilderness program cost around $10,000, and the boarding school cost $43,000. We paid some by credit card, some through my flex spending account, and some cash.

Fourteen months later, Celia, another daughter of Don's, went into another residential treatment center. She was unable to finish the program due to safety concerns by the staff. She was self-harming and needed to be watched 24/7. We got a refund from the program for the weeks she was unable to finish. Boarding school was $5,000 a month, and she was there about a year. Total cost for all of her treatment was approximately $70,000. Again, we paid by cash, credit card, and monthly payments to each place. Eventually, Don had to get student loans for $30,000 each to help cover the cost of both girls' treatment. At one point, we were making payments to seven treatment facilities, paying student loans, plus paying for our weekly therapy sessions. Total mental health monthly payments were around $2,500, which was more money than I brought home each month. I started working two jobs to help us pay the bills.

When the girls were in treatment, Don was acting out sexually, and he was very out of control. He charged around $50,000 on credit cards that he had secretly obtained and was having the bills go to his office. Those monthly payments were about $400 to $500. Don filed for bankruptcy, but I did not. He erased all of his credit debt, along with any debt remaining with the treatment facilities that had not been paid through student loans or credit cards. Thirty-six thousand dollars had been charged on my credit card, and since it was in my name and I did not file bankruptcy, we continued to pay $650 a month on my credit card.

In 2006, Don disclosed to me that he had made $20,000 on a case in which he had assisted an attorney. He originally told me he made $1,500 and gave me that much money to put into the bank. He spent $16,000 on his sex addiction and $2,500 on a new computer that he told me his boss gave him for Christmas. He had cashed in all of his retirement and spent it on sex, borrowed money from his boss to spend on sex, and was making fraudulent loans against his boss for sex money. He had about three car wrecks in the past year and received money to make the car repairs, but instead spent the money on sex. I realized it was never going to end, and I asked him to move out.

It has been a year and a half since I've been separated from Don, and my life continues to improve. I now have only $18,000 in debt and am quickly gaining ground. My recovery program has made all the difference in my life.

In healthy and high-level functionality, partners consult with each other in the area of finances, and both partners have input regardless of the income contribution of either. During recovery in Co-Sex Addicts Anonymous, a woman will learn how to assert her responsibility as co-manager of their funds. She also maintains responsibility for her own checking account, sharing the bill paying and knowing the expenses of the family. There is also appreciation given to both partners for the contributions they provide, whether financial, emotional, or both.

EXAMPLE: After several years prior to recovery of not having her voice in financial and house affairs, Jeannine finally took her power back. It was time for her to have a new car, and she initiated this conversation with Warren. In that conversation, she informed him that she intended to purchase a car of her choice and handle the details of the transaction on her own. She reviewed the financial situation and informed Warren of her intention to spend a certain amount of money on the vehicle of her choosing. While Warren expressed his discomfort with letting go of the control of this purchase, his recovery taught him to let go. He then offered his support and encouragement. For the first time in their marriage, she purchased a luxury vehicle on her own. Jeannine did the research, made the purchase, and has enjoyed this car a great deal.

Some addictive dynamics around money may include the co-sex addict being on the other extreme of financial management. In these cases, the co-sex addict is the primary income earner, manager of the home, primary child caretaker, and is dealing with a noncontributing sex addict. Some authentic relationships do have house fathers or male house managers and men who are the meal planners and primary caretakers of the children in the daytime. The key is that both partners are empowered in the financial decision-making processes and household management affairs. Conscious decision making with equal input by both partners empowers the relationship. Appreciation for both partners is also important. This openness, clarity, respect, and honesty also will determine the level of functionality and authenticity in the partnership.

8

Religious Addiction Versus Healthy Spirituality

*H*ealthy spirituality is the cornerstone of authentic relationships. We believe that many people confuse religion and spirituality. *Religion* is a specific system including beliefs and worship practices often involving a specific code of ethics and particular set of rules and rituals. *Spirituality* is a unique and individualized set of practices and beliefs that individuals choose for themselves. This may or may not include some religious practices. The primary purpose of spirituality is to connect people with their Higher Power, according to their understanding of that Higher Power.

Religious addiction stands in the way of a couple's ability to have an authentic relationship. It also stands in the way of an individual's connection with herself or himself. It prevents someone from being in touch with her feelings and being in reality. As with any addiction, it is a mind-altering behavior. Religious addiction or religiosity is also one of the most difficult addictive behaviors to recognize, since "being religious" is generally valued in our culture.

We define *religious addiction* as the rigid adherence to a set of values and beliefs that provide a way to deny or avoid reality, especially when abusive and harming behaviors are present in the family system.

EXAMPLE: Renata was married to a man who was raised in a strict fundamentalist religious family. He went to church every Sunday and once during the week, and he stayed involved in fund raising and other church activities. He also prayed at every meal and at night-time, and insisted that the family join him. His actions in the home did not often reflect his religious beliefs.

When he and Renata would have conflicts, his behavior would become verbally and emotionally abusive. He would often call her names and belittle and shame her. This was a huge place of pain for her and very confusing. At church and in the outside community, he looked like an upstanding citizen. He was charming and generous. At home, however, he would often rage and use control as the primary way of relating rather than being vulnerable, honest, and loving, as was taught in the doctrines of the church he attended.

Renata had a spiritual connection through her Christian church as well, and for her, there was a huge discrepancy between how Christ might behave and the way her husband treated her. This inconsistency, in his behavior and the teachings of their church, and the continued emotional abuse kept them from having an authentic relationship. Renata's husband stayed actively involved in his church, but refused to stay active in 12-step recovery. He refused to change his raging behaviors and quit marriage and family therapy. The marriage eventually ended in divorce.

As with any addiction, we avoid our feelings by mood altering with a substance or behavior. We also know that an open heart and our feelings are the gateway to closeness and connection. Religious rigidity and religious addiction are techniques used to pull us out of our hearts and feelings, which results in avoiding closeness and connection. This addiction assists in keeping us in denial and in fantasy thinking. Religious addiction keeps a Higher Power/God/Spirit out of the relationship and puts rules, control, and unhealthy rituals in its place.

EXAMPLE: Marion grew up in a Catholic family. She loved many of the beautiful rituals and practices, and she took them with her into her co-sex addiction recovery program. She also learned a lot about the disease of alcoholism, codependency, and other addictive behaviors and incorporated the 12 steps into her spiritual practices.

Her grandmother used religion as an avoidance behavior. Marion's aunt and cousin were active drug addicts, alcoholics, and unrecovered co-sex addicts. Marion attended 12-step meetings to assist her with her codependency with these family members and often invited her grandmother to attend with her. Her grandmother refused and often said she was "praying for them" and that God would make them well. She said the rosary for her daughter and granddaughter. She also enabled their acting out by giving them money and helping to clean up the messes they made while on their binges with drugs and men. This was also her grandmother's way to avoid her pain about the situation. Going to Al-Anon meetings and looking at her enabling behaviors* was a way to deal with the situation and be in reality, but it required her to feel her pain about the situation and accept her powerlessness as well. Her grandmother chose to compulsively pray, say the rosary, and read her religious books instead. This was a way to avoid her real pain inside and create an illusion of control.

Oftentimes, religious addiction can sometimes look good on the outside as an additional cover-up of the pain and emptiness on the inside. Dressing up, volunteering, and getting acknowledgments for chairing committees and teaching Sunday school can be a way to avoid dealing with the sex addiction within the family. It can also be a place to try to tidy up the outside when the inside feels so out of control.

A personal connection with a Higher Power is necessary on the road to authentic relationships. However, we ask that everyone look at their faith and reflect on whether there is an authentic connection with the Spiritual Source of our choosing or if religiosity is a barrier in our relationships.

Authentic spirituality is a personal connection with Spirit, Higher Power, God, and so on. We further believe that this connection comes only after a significant amount of family of origin healing has taken place. The co-sex addict tends to make the addicts in her life "God," and in particular, her father. As an adult, she will put her partners and/or husband in that place. There may have been abuse or unhealthy practices that occurred within religious institutions as well. The leaders in those religious institutions may have taken that role of "God" in her life. Abuse may have occurred in these religious institutions/schools, as has been revealed through sexual abuse in many Catholic organizations around the world. This abuse may be sexual, physical, emotional, spiritual, or any combination of the above.

When a young girl is sexually, emotionally, or physically abused by an addict while she is growing up, there is a dynamic that gets set in place. This painful dynamic may cause her to consistently give away her power to the men in her life, including giving undue authority to her father, priest, or minister and/or eventually her partner. She is looking to heal that original hurt and has become a victim in her life, not finding her power within but looking outside of herself for that power. It is also important for the co-sex addict to reflect upon her present-day situation to see if she has recreated her partner as her Higher Power or if a minister, priest, or religious leader has taken that role in her life.

The awareness of this abuse must take place and be healed in order to create a genuine connection with a Higher Power. Since the foundation of 12-step recovery is having a Higher Power of one's own understanding, individuals may be advised by their sponsors to "fire" their old god and accept a new Higher Power based on their own understanding and new-found values. This connection is the foundation of healthy spirituality. Authentic spirituality has a way of creating fullness on the inside that reflects on the outside a genuine honesty and an ability to connect with ourselves, our Higher Power, and others.

9

Isolation Versus Mutually Empowering Connections with Other Women

Co-sex addiction affects every area of a woman's life, including how she relates to other women. In our disease, we are set up to compare ourselves to other women, see them as competition for the available men, and often treat them with disdain and envy.

One of the issues women experience as a result of being set up as co-sex addicts is this sense of competition they feel with one another. There is conditioning from a very young age to overfocus on being "nice" and "looking good." One cannot go through any day in our American culture without seeing somewhere in the media a "perfectly" shaped woman. Our ads, billboards, magazines, television commercials, and so on generally have well-proportioned and beautiful females. We sell cars, perfume, clothes, beer, and most consumer products with women in the background, scantily dressed, often with unrealistically "perfect" bodies. This focus on appearance conditions young girls to grow up concerned primarily with how they look, not how they think or how powerfully they take care of themselves, earn an income, express their creativity, or make a contribution to others.

Before recovery, there is also conditioning in our culture that tells women they must depend on a man for survival. There is sometimes a spoken and sometimes an unspoken cultural belief that puts the focus on the man's ability to think and a women's ability to look good. We typically look to men to solve our problems.

Even when a woman is being offended by a man, the other women involved in the situation will often side with the man. This is part of a dynamic in which the "offender" is protected and the "victim" is blamed, even for the abuser's behavior.

EXAMPLE: One day Maryann was driving through a parking lot, and a car to her left came around the corner and began to turn into her. There was a near collision and both stopped. Maryann, who had the right of way, could not move forward as the cars were at such an angle that she would have hit the other driver's vehicle. The man, who was clearly not yielding to her right of way, refused to back up and yelled to her to move forward.

After ten minutes of no movement and arguing back and forth, a woman came out of the store in the parking area and yelled at Maryann, "Move your car; he isn't doing anything to you!" A few minutes later, another woman did the same thing, yelling at Maryann and ignoring the fact that she was not at fault and was clearly unable to move forward.

Finally, she attempted to move forward an inch. It was finally clear to the male driver and the others watching that she would hit him. He got into his car, backed up a few inches, and they were on their way.

This example is a general overview of what occurs in our relationships with one another, woman to woman, when we are in our co-sex disease. The dynamic that occurs is that the offender, often the male sex addict, is seen as the "hero" and enabled to be the abuser and use his power to manipulate for sex, control, and so on. The woman is the victim and really has no allies, as the women in the system who are in the midst of their disease will tend to side with the men, even when the men's behavior is abusive and offensive.

In recovery, we learn to solve our own problems and find our value from within, rather than depend on a man for these things. We also begin to see other women as allies and support in our living independent lives rather than as competition for the men we "need."

We believe that the original learning of co-sex addiction takes place in our families of origin. As girls growing up, we learn how to behave from our mothers, grandmothers, aunts, and other female role models in our lives. When we get into co-sex addiction recovery, we begin to realize that the women in our lives were themselves co-sex addicts and taught us those behaviors. Rather than seeing our mothers, grandmothers, and aunts con-front the inappropriate and offensive behaviors of our fathers, grandfathers, and so on, we saw them model their sexual codependency. They dressed to please their sex addicts or the other sex-addicted men of the family. They may have minimized and excused verbal, physical, or sexual overt or covert abuse. They also may have contradicted their own value systems by behaving in ways the addict demanded, leaving them consistently feeling demeaned and victimized.

EXAMPLE: Serena shared her experience of going through a thera-peutic separation within their home from her sex addict husband while in recovery. When her parents came to visit, her mother expressed concern when she saw them sleeping in separate bedrooms. Although Serena did not give much information about the reason for the tempo-rary in-home separation, her mother was quick to express her concern. Serena's mother told her that the way to keep a marriage together was to provide a lot of sex to your husband in whatever ways pleased him. By behaving this way, you could minimize or even possibly prevent your husband from "straying" outside of the home. Serena's mother could not imagine how a separation would keep Serena's husband happy and the marriage strong. In her conditioning, providing sex often was one of the ways to control the husband's acting outside the marriage.

Here is an example of how the mother models enabling the addict and teaches her daughter to be a co-sex addict by trying to control the addict's acting-out behavior with sex without regard to her needs, wants, and values in the marriage. It further establishes the belief that women's role is to provide sex and to keep and control their husbands from being with other women. We do not believe it is a woman's responsibility to "keep her husband from acting out," as is the case with Serena's mother.

Again, this clearly sets up the belief early on that other women are adversaries rather than allies and support in our lives. If Serena's mother holds this belief at this stage of her life, we can assume that this conditioning occurred on a regular basis during Serena's growing-up years and in her cultural upbringing.

Another belief we have is that when a woman grows strong and reclaims her own personal power as an individual, she may experience rejection by other women. In society at large, or even in some recovery circles, a woman with her own voice, strong boundaries, and a view different from the norm can easily be viewed as a threat to the other women. Often this occurs unconsciously in circles of women. It is important to bring it into consciousness so that strong women are appreciated and respected rather than scapegoated or treated with disdain.

In recovery, we will find ourselves using the 12 steps and tools to learn how to develop healthy friendships with women, as well as healthy respect and closeness with them. Being sponsors in a co-sex addicts 12-step program and being sponsored allows us to find a new model for healthy mothering and authentic connections with other women. This relearning of healthy mothering and women-to-women support is a dynamic necessary for the continued growth of Co-Sex Addicts Anonymous internationally.

10

Characteristics of Authentic Relationships and Recovery

uthentic relationships are what we all long for and what our recovering relationships can bring. From our experience, we believe that individuals in a relationship must have a full commitment to their individual self-recovery as a prerequisite to an authentic relationship with someone else.

We believe that something we call *authentic reality* must come first. Authentic reality is based on who you really are with a complete and honest knowledge of your family of origin. An individual who is not honest about her/his family of origin cannot be in an honest, authentic relationship with themselves, and therefore cannot be in an authentic relationship with another human being. This does not mean we disown our family of origin or our herstories. It does mean we accept the reality of our family of origin and our histories.

We also look at what roles we played in our family. After our individual family of origin work, we begin to learn what intimacy is and how we can create intimacy in our lives. In our primary relationships, marriages, and committed relationships of any kind, we need to learn about what authentic intimacy really is and what it is not. We have been confused about this prior to recovery. Our addictive thinking tells us that sex is all there is to love and intimacy. In our sexual codependency, we believe that having sex and taking care of our partner cements the relationship. If we have a relationship, we think we are complete.

Most of the time in the midst of our disease, we thought that if we did sex "right," or if we did it frequently enough, we would have intimacy. Our addictions and addictive thinking took over the relationship. The self-centered part is about believing sex will fix whatever is uncomfortable for us. The codependent part is being willing to be sexual to feed the other's self-centeredness in hopes of filling our own emptiness with their approval. Sex is not intimacy, no matter what our addiction tells us. So this is one of the first things we need to look at and rebuild in our own value system and in our relationship.

When the tools and techniques of this book are utilized, our experience teaches us that transformation will occur, especially within ourselves and our primary relationship. Our sexual expression becomes a spiritual expression, a means to connect on a soul level with our entire being and that of another.

Authentic sexual relationships lead to joy, intimacy, pleasure, and ecstasy that moves us deeply. We are left empowered as individuals by the sexual experience. We experience a closer connection to ourselves and to our partner.

This is different from addictive sexual relating (sex and co-sex addiction) when individuals leave the sexual experience minimized and empty due to their conscious or unconscious attempts to use one another sexually to fill the emptiness within.

Sometimes it is suggested that we stop having sex for a period of time, setting aside that time to learn how to be intimate by sharing our feelings with each other. This separation from the addictive patterns in the relationship may include separate bedrooms and/or separate domiciles. Learning genuine emotional intimacy first and then developing the sexual connection later is the order of authentic relationships.

During the separation, we also reclaim our bodies and our right to say yes or no to our partner regarding sex. We also begin to look at our own desire for sexual connection. In our disease, we automatically became sexual at our partner's request. Now is the time to hold that sensual and sexual energy within our own beings and learn about authentic choice and expression in sharing it with another.

In our recovery, we are able to choose our place in our family, both past and present, rather than being enslaved by our old setup roles. It also means that we find our worth from within ourselves and from turning our lives and will over to our Higher Power. We also identify our own values from which we learn to live our lives.

Genuine intimacy is about sharing all of who we are, including our joys, fears, boundaries, anger, and dreams. Our sexual expression comes from this knowledge and the trust that begins to be built within our partnership from this sharing.

Lovingly hugging, holding hands, and kissing, but not having sex, are behavior changes we make to begin developing more authentic and intimate relationships with ourselves and our partners. We realize that these nonsexual expressions of intimacy had been lost in our addictive patterns. As we begin to experience authentic intimacy in the form of sharing our feelings, thoughts, and nonsexual affection, we create the foundation of authentic, intimate connection. Once we have established the difference between sex and intimacy, we end this time of separation and begin to live a life of authentic relationships.

Real love in our authentic relationships is being consistently caring toward one another without codependency. Sometimes in our recovery from codependency, we think we should do nothing for our partners. And sometimes if we have been in a codependent relationship, we may have to go to the other extreme and do very little for a while. Eventually we find a balance and learn that we can show our love with caring acts or doing for each other when asked. Expressing joy enhances our partnership. The appropriate sharing of these feelings with our mates leads to further intimacy.

Being aware of our partner's needs and wants concerning sex is important in recovery and in developing authentic relationships. We can generally achieve that knowledge through knowing what our own wants and needs are. This opens the door to our partners being aware of their own needs and wants in the area of sexual intimacy. This takes practice, lots of self-knowledge, and recovery work.

CONFRONTATION AS THE ENTRYWAY TO INTIMACY

Confrontation is also a tool used for developing intimacy and authentic relationships. Surprise! When we take the risk to be vulnerable in confronting the other's disease in a loving way, we will find another road to authentic relationships.

At first it may take a lot of healthy anger to learn to confront. Anger gives us the strength and power to confront when our boundaries are being disrespected. Anger also provides the energy and strength to confront when we are overtly or covertly being blamed for another's behavior. This is a dynamic we see often between co-sex addicts and sex addicts. In their respective diseases, the sex addict will avoid responsibility through verbally blaming and manipulating the co-sex addicts into thinking she is the cause of his behaviors and choices. The co-sex addict then takes on this "lie" that she is somehow responsible for her addict's behavior and that she can control him through her own behavior.

The co-sex addict's healthy anger helps her to confront inappropriate behavior and hold the boundaries that she has developed as a way to care for herself. This healthy anger also empowers her to clearly see her part without taking on responsibility for her sex addict's behavior and teaches her how to trust her own intuition.

Our recovery also distinguishes healthy anger from rage. It shows us that rage is not appropriate in confrontation. Shame can turn a good, clean feeling of anger into rage, which is inappropriate. Over time, we learn how to embrace and channel our healthy anger into self-care and care of our relationship. We do shame and emotional healing work so that rage becomes less and less a part of our healthy anger.

Healthy anger and skills in confrontation give way to our reclaiming the knowing part of us that guides us in setting boundaries. It is our belief that boundaries are a necessary component of authentic and intimate relationships. When we learn how to say yes and how to say no, we each achieve one more step toward authentic relationships. We reclaim our ability to choose, particularly in the area of sexuality. The power to fully choose creates safety, empowerment, and self-esteem for the individuals within the relationship; it also creates the foundation for an authentic and thriving partnership.

Self-honesty will reap great results in our recovery and healing. Our experience tells us that working a 12-step program, having a sponsor, doing service work, and doing our own family of origin/grief work will lead us to a place where we can meet another and have an authentic relationship. It is also important to know that sometimes our journey will lead us out of a dysfunctional relationship so we can be ready for a functional and loving relationship with a sober and available partner. While we think this is the most challenging inner work that we will ever do, we also believe the joy, spiritual connection, and fulfillment that we achieve is well worth the journey.

11

Co-Sex Addiction
Resources for Recovery

*W*e have learned that progress in healing from our co-sex addiction happens one day at a time, with mistakes and setbacks along the way. This is an opportunity to learn compassion for ourselves and others. In our co-sex addiction recovery, we walk through our shame and perfectionism by learning through our experience that while we may make mistakes during our recovery journey, we are not a mistake. We learn to allow others to love and support us when we may not be able to love and support ourselves. Through this journey, we learn self-love. Authentic self-love comes when we embrace our imperfections and wounds with kindness and compassion.

This chapter offers various forms of support in recovery from co-sex addiction. These guides may be used for formally writing our 12 steps out and learning more about the tools and techniques to support us in our continued healing and transformation. We are grateful for the 12 steps of Alcoholics Anonymous and 12 promises from the *Big Book of Alcoholics Anonymous*, upon which we have created the steps and promises for co-sex addiction. We also include signs of relapse, which help us to identify when we have fallen back into our disease and indicate where recovering actions are necessary to get back on track.

12 STEPS OF CO-SEX ADDICTION

1. Admitted we were powerless over our co-sex addiction disease and others' sex addiction and that our lives had become unmanageable.

2. Came to believe in a Power greater than ourselves that could restore us to sanity.

3. Made a decision to turn our will and our lives over to the care of this Power as we understand it.

4. Made a searching and fearless moral inventory of ourselves.

5. Admitted to ourselves, our Higher Power, and another human being the exact nature of our wrongs.

6. Became entirely ready to have our Higher Power remove all these defects of character.

7. Humbly asked our Higher Power to remove our shortcomings.

8. Made a list of all people we had harmed and became willing to make amends to them all.

9. Made direct amends to such people whenever possible except when to do so would injure them or others.

10. Continue to take personal inventory, and when we are wrong promptly admit it.

11. Sought through prayer and meditation to improve our conscious contact with our Higher Power, praying only for the knowledge of our Higher Power's will and the courage to carry it out.

12. Having had a spiritual awakening as a result of these steps, we carried this message to others and practiced these principles in all areas of our lives.

Step 1: Admitted we were powerless over our co-sex addiction disease and others' sex addiction and that our lives had become unmanageable.

The first step is both a blessing and a curse. There is such relief, and sometimes even joy, when we are able to finally "get" and "admit" that we are powerless over whatever it is we are struggling with in our lives. Acknowledging our powerlessness over our own behavior and that of others gives us somewhere to go. It is the beginning of seeking help.

In our co-sex addiction disease, walking away from our identity as a victim has been a long and eventful journey. There is a part of us that still wants to blame someone else for our circumstances or our current plight in life. "If he would just stay abstinent, if she weren't so judgmental, if only he, if only she, if only, if only . . . if only . . ."

Embracing the first step and our own powerlessness means that we no longer have someone else or something else to blame. As we move on from the first step, we will eventually come to acknowledge that we consistently have a choice in whatever dilemma or plight lies before us.

Sometimes it is easier to play the victim than it is to be honest, set a boundary, or look into the mirror at our part, but there is always a choice that we make. Now, in recovery, we are responsible for the situations, relationships, and circumstances in our lives. When we admit what we are powerless over, we are able to then see with clarity the choices that lie before us.

Acknowledging our powerlessness and then embracing our own power is the greatest paradigm of the first step. In the vulnerable act of surrender, solutions and even miracles await from a Power greater than ourselves.

As we begin the first step of our co-sex addiction recovery, we start to embrace and feel our feelings. As we spend time looking at our past, doing our grief work, and understanding our powerlessness over the disease, we begin to integrate our emotional selves. A good first step is to do a biography of our lives to fully understand what really happened to us and how powerless we were as victims in the family system.

One of the aspects of ourselves that confronting the disease reveals is how we use controlling behavior. We try to keep from feeling the effects of the disease and our pain by a variety of controlling behaviors. These may include:

- raging and/or withdrawing and isolating
- using sex or lack of it as a control mechanism to get what we want
- snooping, stalking, or hiring a detective (or turning into one ourselves)
- compulsive dieting, compulsive exercising, and so on; forcing ourselves or other members of our family to look "perfect"
- covering up or "cleaning up the mess" left by the sex addict
- drinking, overeating, overspending, use of prescription drugs, marijuana, and so on to cover the pain of our disease
- religious addiction, over-involvement with church, church leaders, or volunteerism to keep us from looking at the reality of our own lives
- compulsive cleaning or passive-aggressive behaviors such as chronic lateness, messiness, lack of organization, and so on
- trying to control our children and their relationships with others

When we admit our powerlessness over this disease and honestly look at the unmanageability of our lives, we are truly at the beginning of our recovery journey. Now it is time for Step 2. We are not alone.

Step 2: Came to believe in a Power greater than ourselves that could restore us to sanity.

The second step asks us to look at how we perceive our Higher Power. Looking at our childhood, we see how our faith was or was not formed. Sometimes it will be healthy, but often we are set up to be religious addicts or to make religion our god. This sets us up to have a relationship with the religion and often leaves out our Higher Power and a personal connection to a Higher Power. We are taught about rules and rituals of a church, leaving us void of a personal relationship with our God.

Another dysfunctional pattern that may occur in our family of origin is the void of any connection to spirituality. This further sets up the addictive connection with the addict or addicts in our family and our dependence on them.

For co-sex addicts who have been raised by unrecovered co-sex addicts and sex addicts, we often see the father sex addict as our Higher Power. Sometimes it can be a grandfather who is set up as the "god" in the family. This sets us up to seek out sex addicts in our adulthood, and then they become our Higher Power. Our entire lives we have been leaving out our true God and treating our sex addicts as God. This plays a part in our setup as co-sex addicts. As we look at this when we hit bottom in co-sex addiction, we are amazed at how this dynamic has happened in our lives.

The second step helps us to look at our lives and become willing to accept our true God and see the sex addict in a new way. We also look at what our co-sex addiction has cost us in the area of spirituality. As we understand this dynamic, a search for a true connection to our Higher Power begins. This connection through the 12 steps shows us the way to faith and authentic spirituality.

EXAMPLE: For Ellen, this dynamic was true. She found herself enmeshed in her family of origin and in her present family. After she became aware of her actions as a co-sex addict, she was startled to see that her religion was her faith base and not her Higher Power, which she called God. As she had this revelation, she felt very lonely and scared. She began searching for her God. The first place she found God was when she was led to a treatment center to look at her co-sex addiction. She had never heard of a treatment center for co-sex addiction, so being in one felt miraculous.

She was able to truly feel her feelings and uncover her anger at the sex addicts in her life. The father sex addict did not have religion or God in his life, so she felt responsible to be very religious to save him. Her mother had the sex addict on a pedestal as her god. When she married a sex addict, she became a convert to his religion. After a few years, his religion felt addictive, and the church seemed male-dominated and unfair to women and gays.

Ellen was unable to get out at that time. During treatment she was able to do written work around the second step which explained her setup, that religion had become her Higher Power, leaving out her authentic God.

Through the second step, she was able to see how this dynamic worked to set up her sex addict husband as her god. In recovery, Ellen was able to find her Higher Power, have a personal relationship with God, and get out of the organized religion that was unhealthy for her.

Today, as she follows the 12 steps, she is able to honor the true God without her codependency with her god—her husband. This allowed for an authentic connection with her husband. Both partners have a personal God/Higher Power and are able and willing to honor each other's spiritual paths.

The second step helps us discover our true God and how to be open to an authentic spiritual experience with our Higher Power. In doing this, we find ourselves and authentic relationships with others.

All of this showed Ellen how her co-sex addiction affected her thinking about God and how she accepted her sex addict as "god." Only when she could admit her insanity could her authentic God restore her to sanity. Only then was she able to embrace her authentic Higher Power. This is the promise of the second step.

Step 3: Made a decision to turn our will and our lives over to the care of this Power as we understand it.

An honest and open look at Steps 1 and 2 make all the difference when we get to Step 3. When we are able to acknowledge and fully embrace the powerlessness of our lives and unmanageability of our disease and others, we may be left with a sense of hopelessness and despair. Moving into Step 2 and believing that there is a Power greater than ourselves that can restore us to sanity is a great relief. Finally, making a decision to turn our will and lives over to that Power is transformational.

There is great freedom in being able to truthfully release our disease and another's into the loving care of a Higher Power. Most people refer to their Higher Power as God, but some may choose not to for various spiritual beliefs or reasons. At this point, we encourage individuals to choose what works for them, so their release and surrender can be authentic and safe.

Making the decision to turn our will and lives over to a Higher Power takes courage. Our co-sex addiction disease is willful, and we have been living our lives as though we can control the disease. This is why Step 1 is so important, so that we can understand our powerlessness. A wise and experienced sponsor is a great help in looking at how we allow our willfulness and fantasy thinking to control our lives. We also look at how we attempted to control the lives of others.

In the midst of our co-sex addiction, and compulsive and obsessive thinking and behavior, we may say the first three steps or Step 3 over and over again. It may be a daily surrender, hourly, or, when in severe pain, minute by minute.

The good news is that this step and the steps prior to it are with us at any moment when we may need or want to embrace them. In letting go and turning our will and lives over to the care of our Higher Power, we are free to experience peace and joy.

Step 4: Made a searching and fearless moral inventory of ourselves.

First, we want to explain what is meant by an inventory. Taking inventory in this step means to look at our lives and the deepest part of our being. During this part of our journey, we look at all the bad actions and thoughts that we have kept hidden, sometimes even from ourselves.

This is the time to see if we have valuable morals and if we have abided by them. Also, it is very important to take an inventory of all of our good actions and thoughts as well. Sometimes we focus only on the bad while hiding the good. This step asks for inventory that is inclusive of good and bad. Sometimes we become martyrs to the co-sex disease and only find the bad that the sex addict focused on in our lives. When staying in our martyr role, we embrace a shame/victim belief that keeps us in our co-sex addiction disease. Shame feeds addiction and keeps it alive.

Our work in Step 4 is enhanced and becomes less self-effacing when we have a sponsor to guide us. Having another woman who we are beginning to trust makes the fourth step less stressful. If you do not have a sponsor, get one. Your life will be changed forever. Having another woman available to you in a nonshaming way is one of the gifts of the program.

In our past lives, we have been preoccupied with our addiction to men and may find few loving and caring women in our lives. Stop and celebrate, for your recovery from co-sex addiction leads you away from the preoccupation with sex addicts and into authentic relationships with your sisters in recovery.

A sponsor and your co-sex addiction sisters will be there for you whenever you ask. You can walk through your past and be honest with yourself and others in the fourth step. Instead of a shaming parent, you have, through your sponsor, a nonshaming and loving sister who has felt the same feelings as you concerning co-sex addiction. To be a sponsor, she will have worked her fourth step with her own sponsor and will know what it is about, thus making her available to you.

Looking at our past and embracing the knowledge of what our co-sex addiction is can more easily be embraced by knowing we have done the third step: turning our life and will over to a Higher Power as we understand it. Then we can face the truth, knowing God's power can enable us to take an honest look at ourselves.

In the fourth step inventory, we look at our part in our relationships: our resentments, places we try to control others, our avoidance of boundary setting, our enabling, and so on. In this step, we look at our behavior, including how we have allowed ourselves to be victimized.

We need to take time to see that part of ourselves that is good, even though addicted. We need to list the things that we like the most about ourselves. Often this can be harder than finding the bad, but we can become fearless in our honesty. Rigorous honesty and bringing to light the secrets we have hidden for so long will bring freedom and joy.

Step 5: Admitted to ourselves, our Higher Power, and another human being the exact nature of our wrongs.

Step 5 provides much freedom for anyone willing to be honest and take action. In Step 4, we discovered in our written inventory what needs to be brought into the light. We learn what needs to be admitted to ourselves, our Higher Power, and to another human being. When we begin to break the silence of our isolation and denial and get down on paper the grief, anger, and pain we have been carrying, the door of hope and possibility opens to us. We see that our lives might be different, and we no longer have to lead lives of quiet desperation. We no longer try to control everything around us or deny the truth of the addictive patterns we've lived with for so long. Step 4 naturally leads us into Step 5 and into the light of honest living.

Admitting to ourselves that we need help, that our pain is real, and that we desire a new way of living is the beginning. Next, we are able to reach out to a Higher Power so that the overwhelming loneliness we have carried for so long can be eased. The last part of Step 5 is speaking it aloud to another human being. Having our sponsor or someone else familiar with the 12-step healing process listen to us with love and compassion is a great comfort. We are breaking the silence of the addictive patterns that we have recreated in our current lives, as well as breaking the silence of our addict patterns set up and learned in our families of origin. We walk through the shame and fear that have kept us locked in denial and isolated us from genuine intimacy with others. For some of us, this may be the first time we have opened ourselves to such honest revelations and had the experience of kind, compassionate acceptance from another person. It may be our first experience of authentic intimacy.

Speaking honestly about the secrets we've held deep within creates a breakthrough in our hearts and minds. We now have a new path to walk so that we never have to return to the old way of living. Whenever we break the denial and speak honestly about our addiction and our family patterns, we directly confront the voices and experiences of shame that keep us quiet and in our addiction. Shame is the fuel that keeps our addictive patterns of thinking, feeling, and behavior in place. Honesty dramatically breaks these shame-based patterns of living.

We have the experience of reaching out to a Higher Power greater than ourselves. We have also begun an honest relationship with ourselves and have spoken it aloud to another human being. These three components allow us the courage and support to move forward in our journey. Step 6 moves us deeper into looking at our part and how to reach out for help in changing our behavior.

Step 6: Became entirely ready to have our Higher Power remove all these defects of character.

Steps 4 and 5 help us to be ready for Step 6. This step is all about becoming ready. There is a need to embrace all of our defects of character, as well as our positive attributes. Once we have done this, we become ready to allow our Higher Power to remove our defects of character and risk a new way of living.

We also bring to this step the compassion and care of Steps 1–5. In sharing with a compassionate sponsor and looking honestly at our family of origin histories, we realize that any addictive patterns of behavior were our best attempts at surviving. We bring kindness, gentleness, and compassion to ourselves and know that we did the best we could with the limited tools we had.

Sometimes we find ourselves not ready to have these shortcomings removed. Even though our behavior has caused us pain and kept us in our co-sex addiction, it is familiar to us, albeit a sick familiarity. Living our lives without these defects of character and stepping out into the unknown can be frightening. So, at that time, we reconnect with Step 2, which reminds us that we believe in a Higher Power that can restore us to sanity. We realize once again that we are not alone and can rely on our spiritual strength for support and comfort. We can then see the insanity of holding on to our co-sex addiction disease. Holding on to something that is killing us is insanity. So Step 2 says that we believe that our Higher Power can restore us to sanity. With this realization of Step 2, we are willing to release control and become ready for our Higher Power to remove our defects of character.

After reflection on this, Ellen (whose story is given under Step 2) became ready. In fact, she was "dying" to be rid of those co-sex defects of character. She realized that she could not do it alone. This is one of the many spiritual aspects of this program. She could see that she was "dying in addiction" and was unable to give up her old behaviors without a Higher Power's help. She became entirely ready to have her Higher Power remove all these defects of character.

We come to believe, and in so doing, we become ready to do this step.

Step 7: Humbly asked our Higher Power to remove our shortcomings.

On the surface, this may seem like a quick and easy step. However, in our honesty we find that we have become accustomed to an old way of living. Even though it is not healthy, it is familiar to us. Changing our long-standing behaviors and asking for our shortcomings to be removed mean we forge ahead into the unknown.

Can we really let go of our attempts to control? Refrain from taking someone else's inventory? Stop giving advice and manipulating to get our way? Do we really want to risk being rejected by asking directly for our needs and wants? Are we able to humbly ask for our Higher Power's assistance? Others have also become accustomed to our taking care of them. Could our new behaviors and boundaries upset the caretaking and codependency we've carefully crafted?

After we have identified some of our shortcomings and defects of character in Step 6, we ask humbly for assistance from our Higher Power. Many people define humble as "submissive" or "weak." Humble for us means shedding the arrogance of thinking that we can control another's behavior or our own addictive behavior. It allows us to create a partnership with our Spiritual Source, our Higher Power.

We also know that humility is not being a victim or doormat, allowing others to walk all over us. It means standing in the truth and reality that we are a worthy human being, and we're open to our Higher Power's will for us and those we love. With humility we begin to see our valued place in the universe. We no longer need to control outcomes. We begin to use the spiritual tools we are learning rather than relying on our shortcomings and defects of character that we developed to survive in our disease.

Step 7 takes courage as we step into a new way of living. We have the courage to move in this direction as we embrace our partnership with our Higher Power, and honest and authentic relationships with ourselves and others. We humbly ask for our shortcomings to be removed and are then ready for Step 8.

Step 8: Made a list of all people we had harmed and became willing to make amends to them all.

It is very important that we get a pen and paper and *make a list*. Some co-sex addicts anonymous newcomers make the mistake of hearing "we have harmed" and then start to make amends immediately. This step is about looking into your heart and seeing who you have harmed. It requires deep introspection and is not to be acted upon quickly or lightly.

Again, it is wonderful to have a sponsor to work this step with. Since the co-sex addict is generally the victim, some of us step right in to make amends to all of our offenders. Yes, we said "offenders." That is how the co-sex addict victim's mind works. Our sponsor guides us to look at our children, friends, and family to see how our co-sex addiction affects them. After we have written down their names and reflected on how they have been hurt, we look at our offenders. Did our co-sex addiction keep us from confronting their disease so that we became the little offender? In that way, we can offend the offender. So, the offender does go on our list.

We also need to determine who our co-sex addiction hurt the most: ourselves. Our co-sex addiction behavior has demeaned and lowered us in most ways. "I give up me to do for you; I accept unacceptable behavior; I will be sexual when I don't want to be sexual." Having sexual practices that play out our childhood abuse is another way that we demean ourselves as co-sex addicts.

Another way the co-sex addict acts out is when she allows her partner to tell her how and when to have sex. Other examples are allowing our partners to use pornography or lack of accountability. We may allow our partner to hide finances so that we do not confront his attending strip clubs, using pornography, phone sex, Internet sex, or other sexual connections.

These are all ways that our co-sex addict stays mute so that we can have the fantasy of staying connected to our addiction, which is the relationship. This shows us how we hurt ourselves the most. "Me" is generally number one on our list when it comes to making amends.

The last part of the step is about becoming willing. To most of us this is clear after our deep introspection, which leads us to want to be willing. With our Higher Power's help, we can be willing to make amends, and with prayerful guidance from our Higher Power and others in the program, we move on to Step 9, where direct amends take place.

Step 9: Made direct amends to such people whenever possible except when to do so would injure them or others.

In Step 8, we became entirely ready. Now is the time to seek guidance from our Spiritual Source and sponsor to determine when making direct amends is the best action for all involved.

Oftentimes having put ourselves first on the list, we will begin there. Looking at ways that we hurt ourselves and allowed ourselves to be hurt over and over can be painful. We must learn to forgive ourselves in this step. We can also make direct amends in a variety of ways.

When Shannon, a recovering co-sex addict, did this step with her sponsor, she listed her behaviors that hurt herself and then listed amends she would make to herself. For example:

Behavior

- overeating to stuff her feelings
- tolerating verbal abuse

- overfocusing on family

Amends

- exercising three times a week
- setting boundaries and removing herself when the abuse begins

- taking an art class that she wanted to do for years

For each behavior that Shannon identified as hurtful to herself, she listed an amend that contradicted the hurt. These powerful actions made a difference in her journey of self-love and authentic relationships. This intimacy begins with self.

It is important in this step to also go through the amends listed with our sponsor before making direct amends. Sometimes approaching someone from our past may not be in their best interest or ours. Oftentimes, rather than directly communicating with someone, it is better to simply pray for their well-being and find another, more creative way to make amends.

With those closest to us, we may have a conversation to own our behavior and apologize. However, the most powerful aspect of making amends is to also commit to changing our behavior. Continuing to work on ourselves, honestly owning our behavior, and doing our best to practice new behaviors in our lives and with those we love are the greatest amends we can offer.

Step 10: Continue to take personal inventory, and when we are wrong promptly admit it.

This step can help us to be accountable for our behavior as recovering co-sex addicts. We take a mini-inventory once a day to keep in touch with our behavior recovery. Often people will do this in their daily morning meditation, or they may do their inventory last thing before they fall asleep.

We look at our actions and stay honest with ourselves. When we see that we have offended or hurt someone, we make amends immediately, to ourselves and others. In taking an inventory on a regular basis, it is important to incorporate gentleness and kindness. Many co-sex addicts develop a self-abusive, perfectionist attitude with themselves that is shame-based. We make a mistake and see ourselves as a mistake. We hurt ourselves or others and internally beat and berate ourselves for this behavior.

Step 10 is an opportunity to be gentle with ourselves and others. To accept our humanness and imperfections is the gift of this step. We learn to honestly take responsibility for our behavior without harming ourselves or expecting perfection from ourselves. We stay realistic in our expectations and make amends without harming ourselves or allowing harm to come to us in the process.

Step 11: Sought through prayer and meditation to improve our conscious contact with our Higher Power, praying only for the knowledge of our Higher Power's will and the courage to carry it out.

This step is one of the greatest gifts of our recovery. This is a spiritual program. Going to meetings regularly and practicing the 12 steps allows us to maintain our contact with our Higher Power and to put these principles into our lives. It also enhances our self-knowledge, which keeps us growing spiritually and attunes us to our Higher Power's will for us and the willingness and courage to follow through.

Prayer is our opportunity to speak to our Higher Power. Meditation allows us the opportunity to have our Higher Power speak to us and provide us the guidance we seek. Daily meditation and spiritual practices that connect us with our Higher Power are essential in our lives. People have unique and different ways of seeking prayer and meditation to maintain conscious contact. Attending 12-step meetings is a powerful spiritual practice that continues to improve our conscious contact with our Higher Power. Some recovering co-sex addicts find that nature, exercise, journaling, and other self-care behaviors are ways that their conscious contact with their Higher Power is enhanced. In Co-Sex Addicts Anonymous meetings, we begin with prayer and end with prayer, and we do this together with the power of the group and as a public acknowledgment of our spiritual connection. Often recovering co-sex addicts have the experience of having their Higher Power speak through someone else's sharing in the meeting. We believe that attending Co-Sex Addicts Anonymous meetings is one of the most powerful tools for improving our conscious contact with our Higher Power and learning what our Higher Power's will is for us. When important decisions need to be made and our Higher Power's will is sought, it is often best to seek counsel from others in the program. We also learn to sit with the discomfort of not knowing before taking action.

The power of the group gives us the courage to carry out the will of our Higher Power and is an ongoing tool for maintaining our spiritual contact.

Step 12: Having had a spiritual awakening as a result of these steps, we carried this message to others and practiced these principles in all areas of our lives.

The key to this step is a spiritual awakening, which comes to us as a result of working the steps. Our lives have really changed when we have had rigorous honesty. This honesty has led us to look at the only person we can change—and that is ourselves.

These 12 steps give us the blueprint of recovery from co-sex addiction. When we work these steps, we find that our Higher Power is there beside us. One way we work the steps is to get out of our Higher Power's way so that we can be guided and healed. Our Higher Power can guide us to be a messenger when we are in recovery for co-sex addiction. When we practice the principles of our Co-Sex Addicts Anonymous program and other people begin to see us change, it encourages them to begin to change themselves so they can have what we have.

Our spiritual awakening is reflected as we practice the principles of this program, such as patience, honesty, and self-care. We become more available to ourselves and others. We find we need to practice introspection on a regular basis rather than criticism. We practice letting go of control and allowing no one to control us. We daily turn our life over to the care of our Higher Power.

In co-sex addiction recovery, service work is an ideal way to put Step 12 into action. We do this when we sponsor others, lead or chair meetings, volunteer time to do phone work, or take time to speak with newcomers.

We may find that people in our workplace, schools, families, and communities begin to respond to us differently and share more of themselves as we change and grow through our working the steps daily. As we work the program and try to stay attuned to our Higher Power's leading, we may have additional opportunities to share more fully and carry the message to others. It is in this step that we share the principles of the program and our experience in recovery.

12 PROMISES OF CO-SEX ADDICTION

We know from our own commitment to recovery and our experience in using these tools that our lives will be transformed. As we journey through our 12-step co-sex addiction recovery program, we begin to experience these promises and see these miracles come true:

1. We will know a new freedom and experience joyful living.

2. We will fully embrace our past and see how wisdom and maturity grew out of our pain and addictive behavior.

3. We will know peace, serenity, and a genuine connection to ourselves and others.

4. We will share our experience to make a difference in the lives of others.

5. Our lives will be purposeful, and we will grow in self-esteem and self-appreciation.

6. We will gain a healthy interest in our own lives and give to others from a place of fullness within.

7. Our whole attitude and outlook on life will change.

8. We will welcome prosperity in all areas of our lives.

9. We will grow to trust ourselves and learn how to choose trust-worthy people.

10. A healthy sense of fear will guide us in unsafe situations, and our self-confidence will grow.

11. We will intuitively know how to handle situations that once baffled us.

12. We will suddenly realize that our Higher Power is doing for us what we could not do for ourselves.

INDICATIONS OF RELAPSE

First of all, relapse is part of the co-sex addiction disease. We cannot do recovery "perfectly," and so we learn over time to be gentle and forgiving with ourselves. We are not God, and we cannot do this perfectly. Each time we fumble or slip, we have an opportunity to be reminded of our need for a Higher Power. We also come to accept our healthy reliance on our co-sex addiction program and the recovering people in our lives.

Some indications of relapse include:

- Feeling confused, disoriented, and not "centered"
- Obsessing or thinking too much about the addict
- Inability to focus on daily tasks and responsibilities
- Beginning to snoop or check up on the addict
- Isolating and not wanting to have contact with recovery people
- Trying to control others, especially the addict
- Beginning to plan or strategize how to get information about the addict's behavior
- Needing to look for, expect, or want validation and approval from outside of ourselves
- Avoiding meetings, therapy, or other recovery environments and friends
- Engaging in addictive behaviors such as overeating, compulsive shopping, over-volunteering, and so on
- Noticing our own internal criticisms, judgments, and blaming of ourselves and/or others
- General irritability and discontentedness

12

Stories of Authentic Recovery and Powerful Serenity

To demonstrate how the disease of co-sex addiction affects real people's lives and to also demonstrate the transformational gifts of recovery, we offer these stories. We thank each woman who has courageously, willingly, and generously shared her story with us. They have done so for their continued recovery and out of service to all women, especially those who still suffer. Names and detailed information have been changed to protect anonymity and confidentiality.

LEIGH ANN'S STORY

I was born right in the middle of the post–World War II baby boom. Hence, I grew up during a period of profound cultural change in the United States: the birth control pill was becoming widely available, the civil rights movement was taking off, and the Vietnam War was soon to polarize the country. When I was seven, my family moved to a tropical paradise where people spent most of their time at the beach wearing very little clothing and generally living a care-free, hedonistic life. I was a teenager in the 1970s—the era of sex, drugs, and disco. Casual sex was the norm. Virginity was viewed as something to lose sooner rather than later. My girlfriends and I got on the Pill when we were in our midteens.

I think that even if my family had been healthy and functional concerning relationships and sexuality, the times and environment in which I was reared would have been enough to set me up for my co-sex addiction. But my family was far from healthy.

My father was an ex-military officer—demanding, critical, and withholding of affection and approval. He treated my mother like his subordinate officer—"Jane, go tell Leigh Ann she left her wet towel on the floor"—and his own personal Playboy bunny. I found the pho-tographic proof when I was ten. My mother had affairs for as long as I can remember. Some were emotional affairs. Some were sexual. She took me along on some of her dates as her alibi. I remember feeling horribly ashamed and powerless on these trysts. I was betraying my father by going along and not telling him. But I couldn't tell my father and betray my mother. To this day, I think this was one of the cruelest and most selfish things my mother ever did to me. It was also one of the most significant ways in which she set me up to carry her shame about what she was doing. My mother's affairs were the ele-phant in the living room nobody talked about. She worked at night as a hotel receptionist. Her excuse for working nights was that it allowed her to be home for the children, but it also allowed her to go out after work. I remember numerous arguments between my parents about how late at night my mother came home.

I had one older brother. He teased me mercilessly when we were children, and he would invite his friends over to watch him "beat me up." This generally involved forcing me behind heavy living room furniture where I would remain trapped until he decided to free me, hitting me with large cushions, and practicing his karate and judo moves on me. Looking back, I think my brother was acting out my father's rage (his shame and anger) over my mother's behavior. Despite this treatment and the humiliation it caused me, I looked up to him and wanted him to love me and be kinder to me.

When I was twelve, my parents finally separated and divorced. My father's version of what happened was that he finally had had enough. My mother's version was that she had finally found the great love of her life and was willing to give up everything for him, which included me and my brother.

My mother moved back to the country she was from to be with her "one true love." Abandoned, lonely, and frightened, I soon started hanging around with the kids who were already drinking, doing drugs, and having sex. When my brother told me that I was to blame for my parents' divorce, I readily believed him. Although I had always been a good student, my grades began to suffer, and I started getting into trouble at school and at home.

One weekend, I told my father I was spending the night at my girlfriend's house. She told her parents she was staying at my house. In reality, we were both going to spend the night at a boy's house—his family was going away for the weekend. I had a crush on him and was hoping to have sex with him that weekend and finally lose my virginity. I was fourteen years old. My father found out I had lied, and he grounded me for the rest of the summer. He wrote and told my mother what I had done. Several days later, she flew home, planning to take me back to live with her. By the time my mother arrived, I had made amends to my father, I was no longer grounded, and I was back to hanging around with my delinquent friends. This was the time in my life when I started looking to relationships with boys to fix me—to make me feel pretty, acceptable, lovable, and not so terribly lonely.

My dating history can be summed up in a few short sentences: I had sex to get what I really wanted—a relationship, approval, and the feeling of emotional connection. But I always picked unavailable and inappropriate boys and men. When I was in high school, I dated a married man. This relationship continued off and on for three years. I also dated my best friend's older brother—he was a drug addict. Everyone I dated cheated on me. The exception was my first boyfriend in junior high school. He was kind, did well in school, and worshipped me. He drew me pictures, wrote notebooks full of poetry for me, and called me every day after school—and I couldn't stand it. I dumped him for one of the bad boys in school who treated me shabbily. Of course, based on what I witnessed in my family, this seemed much more like love to me.

As soon as one relationship ended, which usually didn't take long, I desperately sought my next fix. I was young and attractive, and not very selective, so it didn't take long. I believed that in order to get a relationship, I had to have sex. But I was afraid that if I had sex with a guy on the first date, then he'd never call again. So I came up with my "second, third, or fourth date" formula—not so soon as to seem slutty, but not so delayed that he'd lose interest first. Even though I felt compelled to have sex, it was terrifying to have sex for the first time. I was afraid of being sexually inadequate or not pretty enough. So I relied on drugs and alcohol to deaden my fear of being physically and sexually intimate. And I turned into a human chameleon. I did whatever my boyfriends wanted. I thought I had to in order to have the relationship. One of my high school friends commented to me even back then that my wardrobe changed with each new relationship, and she was right! I wore whatever my boyfriend wanted me to

READER/CUSTOMER CARE SURVEY

We care about your opinions! Please take a moment to fill out our online Reader Survey at **http://survey.hcibooks.com.**
As a **"THANK YOU"** you will receive a **VALUABLE INSTANT COUPON** towards future book purchases
as well as a **SPECIAL GIFT** available only online! Or, you may mail this card back to us.

(PLEASE PRINT IN ALL CAPS)

First Name   MI.   Last Name

Address   City

State   Zip   Email

1. Gender
☐ Female   ☐ Male

2. Age
☐ 8 or younger
☐ 9-12   ☐ 13-16
☐ 17-20   ☐ 21-30
☐ 31+

3. Did you receive this book as a gift?
☐ Yes   ☐ No

4. Annual Household Income
☐ under $25,000
☐ $25,000 - $34,999
☐ $35,000 - $49,999
☐ $50,000 - $74,999
☐ over $75,000

5. What are the ages of the children living in your house?
☐ 0 - 14   ☐ 15+

6. Marital Status
☐ Single
☐ Married
☐ Divorced
☐ Widowed

7. How did you find out about the book?
(please choose one)
☐ Recommendation
☐ Store Display
☐ Online
☐ Catalog/Mailing
☐ Interview/Review

8. Where do you usually buy books?
(please choose one)
☐ Bookstore
☐ Online
☐ Book Club/Mail Order
☐ Price Club (Sam's Club, Costco's, etc.)
☐ Retail Store (Target, Wal-Mart, etc.)

9. What subject do you enjoy reading about the most?
(please choose one)
☐ Parenting/Family
☐ Relationships
☐ Recovery/Addictions
☐ Health/Nutrition
☐ Christianity
☐ Spirituality/Inspiration
☐ Business Self-help
☐ Women's Issues
☐ Sports

10. What attracts you most to a book?
(please choose one)
☐ Title
☐ Cover Design
☐ Author
☐ Content

TAPE IN MIDDLE; DO NOT STAPLE

BUSINESS REPLY MAIL
FIRST-CLASS MAIL PERMIT NO 45 DEERFIELD BEACH, FL

POSTAGE WILL BE PAID BY ADDRESSEE

Health Communications, Inc.
3201 SW 15th Street
Deerfield Beach FL 33442-9875

FOLD HERE

Comments

wear. It was what I knew—my mother dressed me up in clothes that matched my dolls when I was little, and she had always focused on my appearance more than anything else about me.

A few months before I was to start high school, my mother's lover returned to his wife, and my mother returned to where we lived. Now that she had been left, she was ready to be a mother of sorts again. My father had remarried by this time. He seemed relatively happy. My stepmother had two grown sons from her first marriage, and we were all living together. Things were fairly stable, but I was ready to start high school and wanted to go to school with all my friends. My mother rented an apartment, got a job, and I moved in with her. She made it clear that she didn't want to be my "mother," and that she preferred for us to be more like roommates. And we were. Although she made me do weekly chores, that was about it. When she found out I was dating a married man, she did nothing except comment on how handsome he was. She knew I was smoking pot and drinking. She did nothing. She flirted with my boyfriends, wore sexually provocative clothing around them, and generally made me feel embarrassed and inadequate. To this day, one of the boys I dated then refers to those times as seeming just like the scene in the movie *The Graduate* where Anne Bancroft's character seduces Dustin Hoffman's character. When I finally confronted my mother about her behavior with my boyfriends, her comment was that I should just admit I couldn't compete with her and to stop trying.

When I was eighteen, I started working as a fashion model. I was being dressed up and treated like an object. It felt perfectly normal. By this time, I was living on my own. My mother had remarried and moved away during my senior year in high school, and my father and stepmother had moved to another country. I continued having a series of relationships with men who cheated on me. I traveled throughout Europe and Japan, returning home every few months or so. I was lonely, afraid, and desperately looking for someone who would love me. My mother bragged to all her friends about my "glamorous" life and displayed pictures of me throughout her house. Now that she was older, she was getting less attention from men, and she began to live vicariously through me. When I visited her, she complained that I wasn't wearing makeup and looking like a model. She wanted details about where I traveled, who I dated, and so on.

My father, on the other hand, was disappointed in me—like always, it seemed—and uncomfortable with how I was making a living. That wasn't the only thing he was ashamed of. On my first visit to their house since my father and stepmother had moved away, they asked me to pretend my stepmother was my mother. I guess they were pretending to all their friends that neither one of them had been married before. And one day, when my stepmother and I were alone together, she confided in me that she and my father had never had sex! That was one of the last things I wanted to know about, but I felt powerless to tell her so. So I sat there and listened to her tell me about her frustrations. By this time, I was pretty well trained to accept inappropriate behavior silently.

When I was in my midtwenties, I met a handsome man from a wealthy family. Rex was surely, I thought, my salvation. He was getting a divorce, had one child, was an artist, and enjoyed making big romantic gestures—he once bought me every rose a flower vendor was selling. He was exciting and unpredictable. I moved in with him after our fifth date. It took me a few months to figure out that he was also a full-blown alcoholic who had blackouts and would have been fired from his job if his father didn't own the company. It took me another three years to learn that he really was my salvation, but not like I predicted.

My relationship with Rex led me to recovery. One of his best friends was in Alcoholics Anonymous, and his wife went to Al-Anon. She took me to my first 12-step meeting. I stayed with Rex for a couple of years and continued going to Al-Anon. I got a sponsor. I tried to work the steps. I started going to other 12-step meetings. I stopped drinking and doing drugs. I went to AA meetings for my own drinking and drug use. Rex continued to struggle with his own sobriety, and we finally broke up. I decided not to date for a year. I was happier than I'd ever been. I got into therapy and started really looking at my family history. I started going to Adult Children of Alcoholics meetings even though I couldn't identify an alcoholic in my family. Both my parents drank socially as far as I knew, but I had almost all of the symptoms of children reared in an alcoholic home. I developed healthier relationships with women and started spending more time with women than I ever had before. I stopped viewing other women as competition and a measure by which to judge myself, for better or for worse.

Although my life was going better than it ever had, something was still missing. None of the meetings I attended addressed the compulsive sexual behavior I'd struggled with since I was a teenager. I still felt so much shame about allowing myself to be objectified, my pattern of picking men who betrayed me, and my willingness to have sex so early in a relationship. I had also engaged in risky sexual behavior, which I felt ashamed of, too. One of the more dangerous things I used to do was to perform oral sex on boyfriends while they were driving, not to mention all the unprotected sex.

Finally, I heard about Co-Sex Addicts Anonymous. In those days, one had to be interviewed before being invited to a meeting. That was one interview I nailed! The woman who interviewed me already knew me from other 12-step meetings, and we had become pretty friendly. She and her husband were both in recovery. They were kind, generous, loving, and fun to be with. I adored them. (I still do.)

I would like to say that I felt at home the very first time I went to a Co-Sex Addicts Anonymous meeting, but I didn't. I sat in the meeting room, which wasn't much different from the dozens of other meeting rooms I'd been sitting in by then, and tried to make sense of what the women were saying. I could tell they were speaking English, but it seemed like gibberish to me. My brain wasn't the only thing not cooperating with me being there—my body started to protest, too. I felt panicky and squirmy. It was all I could do to make myself stay through an entire meeting. Luckily, I persevered, the words started making sense, and my panic subsided. Every woman there talked about things I completely understood. Some of the details were different, but the feelings and beliefs that motivated them to act the way they did made perfect sense to me and sounded like my own story.

I got a sponsor and started working the steps—finally. I stayed out of relationships with men for another year. When I did start dating again, I dated Dave, a man I became friends with in another 12-step program. For the first time in my life, I developed a friendship with a man before we ever had sex. And, for the first time in my life, the man I dated wasn't cheating on me. Dave moved in with me about six months after we met—three months after we started dating. We both continued going to meetings, and I continued working on my family of origin and co-sex addiction issues. Dave came from a family that was extremely dysfunctional, and he was estranged from them all. I think he thought that if he just stopped being around them, he could escape the effects of his upbringing.

In the course of getting to know Dave, he told me about his own sexual issues—Internet pornography, mostly. I told him about Sex

Addicts Anonymous meetings, and he started going to them. We went to meetings for couples in recovery. Our relationship wasn't perfect, but it was by far the healthiest relationship I'd ever been in. We were open, we talked about our feelings, and, because I was no longer afraid of being abandoned, I didn't have sex when I didn't want to, like I'd always done in the past.

I went back to college and finished my degree. I graduated with top honors. I got a counseling degree and worked as a counselor for several years. Dave and I married while I was still in college. He was wonderfully supportive and encouraging. I went on to graduate school and again graduated with honors. I landed a very good job in my chosen field and started working hard.

Dave was working hard, too, and he traveled a lot on business. We both gradually stopped going to meetings. We stopped having sex. We stopped talking about our feelings on a regular basis. We went out on "dates" less and less and got into a rut. Day by day, we grew further apart, and that familiar feeling of loneliness and abandonment crept back into my life. I started feeling crazy—his behavior had changed. When he was home, Dave went to sleep in the guest room every night. He told me that because he was trying hard to get a promotion, he was exhausted from working so hard during the week. I told him how miserable and lonely I was, and I threatened that I was either going to leave or have an affair if things didn't change. Dave promised that things would be better once he found out about his promotion. Despite knowing better, I continued staying away from meetings. I told myself I was doing okay, but I was miserable. On more than one occasion I wondered how I could possibly stay in the relationship. Things were bad and getting worse, and I was stuck. I had put my own happiness and contentment on hold while Dave focused on work and financial success. I stopped being responsible for my own happiness and convinced myself that once Dave got the promotion he wanted (and all the money that came with it), he and I would get back to normal, and I'd be happy.

Then one day, I found a water bottle full of vodka hidden in the guest room. When I confronted him, Dave confessed that he was drinking to get to sleep, taking prescription drugs, and acting out with Internet pornography again while he was out of town during the week. Three days later, he was on his way to a treatment center, and I was on my way back to a Co-Sex Addicts Anonymous meeting. I've been going to meetings regularly ever since.

That was about eighteen months ago. Dave and I didn't make it, but I did. The tools I learned from all those years of Co-Sex Addicts Anonymous were still there when I really needed them and was in enough pain to admit that I needed help. I'm single again for the first time in eighteen years, and I'm doing okay. Dave's slip ended up giving me a tremendous gift. It helped me get unstuck. I finally made it back to Co-Sex Addicts Anonymous meetings, back to myself, and back to my own spirituality. Going through the painful dissolution of my marriage has reminded me that happiness is an inside job, and that the tools of recovery are always available when we are ready to put them to use.

MINDI'S STORY

My overall sense of my childhood was that I was incredibly sad, lonely, and full of yearning. If I look at all of my pictures from ages one, two, and older, I am very sad looking and there is emptiness inside.

My father was an immigrant and was obsessed with completing his education and making his way in this culture. I had one sister. She was physically and emotionally abusive, controlling and often overpowered me. No one did anything about the physical and emotional abuse between my sister and me. Although my mother was physically there, I have no memories of her interacting with us, playing, or talking with us. I believe that I was very bright and severely unengaged and neglected in my home environment.

When I was three years old, I figured out how to masturbate. I was so understimulated and masturbating was a way to be stimulated. I also suspect that I may have been sexually abused as a one-year-old when we spent a year with my father's family. I only know that we were there from my mother, not from my own memories. Even if nothing overtly occurred in terms of sexual incest or abuse, I believe that there was a great deal of oppression for women. I feared my paternal grandparents and family in general. The compulsive masturbation continued through my adult life until recovery.

My parents were able to provide physical safety and material security, but were authoritarian. They were critical and shaming as well. Both my sister and I were perfectionists and I grew up feeling less than, ugly and empty inside. I was also told I was the "charming," "quick," and "talented" one so there were many mixed messages from my parents. To compensate, I often projected to the outside that I was carefree and happy.

My sister and I escaped by reading and we read as much as we

could beginning at age four. We knew that there were high expectations of us and we strived to do well academically. Being the only
Asian children in school added to our feeling of shame and "not fit-
ting in." We did not learn from our parents how to socialize in this
American culture. We felt lost and scared a lot.

At home, my father would openly objectify women on television.
I wondered why my mother did not confront him and at the same
time, I took note of what "being attractive" was to men. There was
an obsession with women's looks, and as a family, we would critique
and watch "Miss America" pageants. We openly discussed what was
attractive and what was not. Raging was a regular occurrence at
home and often my father would come home and randomly snap and
scream at us. He would call us stupid, threaten to kill us and rant for
thirty minutes. He would then not speak for several days. I lived in
constant tension and fear.

In school I developed a very "pleasing personality" and strived to
be liked and to get along with everyone. Every year, I would be recognized as the "teacher's pet" and worked hard to be in that position.
My father was grandiose. He would tell us that we were superior to
others so we thought we had to be. Sometimes I would try to get
approval from other kids by doing their work and cheating for them.
Being liked and approved of was a necessity. I strived and was driven
to be recognized in any arena in which approval was possible.

In high school, I was driven to achieve, succeed, and please
others. Physically maturing bodies were a fascination for me. I
learned all about sex in sex education at school. There was no discussion at home about sex and I was consistently masturbating
through this whole time of my life. I would have very long crushes
on boys in school and it was all in secret. I actually did want certain
boys' attention but I could not let anyone know that I had any needs
or wants in that way. I learned to be "needless" and "want less" in my
family from my father. My mother's identity revolved around us and

this seemed needy and pathetic to me. I was disgusted by her neediness and I identified more with my father who seemed to need nothing. I remember feeling highly sexual in high school and wondering if everyone felt this way.

When I went off to college, I was focused on making friends and creating an image for myself. My self-esteem revolved around other's perception of me. I was quite egocentric and narcissistic at this time. I heard through the grapevine that I was desired by many men and it gave me a "high." I liked being an unattainable object of desire. However, at the end of my first year of college, I experienced an instant attraction to a man and I immediately idealized who he was. He was extremely talented, charming and was very self-destructive in his habits. He drank excessively, vandalized property and was unsafe. We were sexual within the first few days of meeting and this was my first experience of sexual intercourse. I noticed how I lost my voice with him. I shut down and could literally not speak with him for fear of doing or saying something wrong that might jeopardize our relationship. I was so afraid of being abandoned and my fear came true. He suddenly stopped calling and I was unable to speak with him about this. I was devastated, but never spoke about it to anyone. In my family, I learned from my father not to "need" or "want" anything so when something happened like the end of the relationship with someone I cared about, I could not talk about it. I obsessed every day for two years about this man.

Finally, a few years later, I met someone else who triggered all my family-of-origin issues. This man was older and like a father figure to me. He was extremely charming, talented, and eccentric, and like my dad, emotionally unavailable. He was distant and because neither of us knew how to connect emotionally or share genuine affection, we both pretended we did not care. I spent a good deal of time fantasizing about the future with him and wanting him to be different and thinking if he was, things would be perfect.

After I entered grad school, I broke up with him and immediately began a relationship with someone else. I chose someone who was young and who I could control. We were compulsive sexually and often had sex three or four times a day. I exercised control and manipulation, and enjoyed having sexual control over this man. There were many facets of this relationship that looked good on the outside, but it was very ego-serving for me.

After graduation with a master's degree, I was home for a short time. I was unsure of my future and very uncomfortable being with my parents. While at college and grad school, I had very little contact with them.

During that period of time, I was twenty-two and would go on hikes and outings with my dad and we began to talk more and more. On one of the hikes, my father would ask personal questions about my sexual activity and boyfriends and I would tell him the details of my relationships. My father told me I was the first person he shared that information with and had even spoken about sex with and this was both scary and flattering to me. I had always felt so desperate to be close to my father and in my disease, this felt like closeness to me, although I confused danger and appropriate intimacy. He also talked about the lack of sexual contact with my mother and spoke to me about how beautiful he thought I was. To finally hear that my father approved of me as a lovely woman was like a drug and a hit of adrenalin to me. He shared with me at that time that if he were a younger man, I would be the woman he would want. Because of how starved I was for fatherly approval, I took this as validation of my worth. My deep emptiness and yearning for acknowledgment was being fed, even though I felt fear and disgust that there was sexual energy between us.

A couple of days after this hike, my father approached me at home. There was the same kind of strange, inappropriate sexual tension between us. He reached over while we were together on the couch and fondled my breast. My mother came home at that time and she began to cook dinner. I followed my father upstairs and even though a part of me did not want to go, I was unable to stop myself. Then we were on his bed and he tried to kiss me and showed me his penis. After this, I got up and left. I was terrified and felt insane. I walked back into his room and told him that he was never to touch me like this again. It was the most horrible feeling and really felt like I was going to go crazy. My world became even smaller and more unsafe.

I left home and moved to another city. Shortly after arriving in this new city, I was at a summer workshop and met my current husband. I was both terrified of him and could not resist him and the relationship became sexual immediately. It was like heroin to a heroin addict. Looking back, I realize that the relationship was extremely addictive. I was utterly powerless over my compulsion to connect with him. There was no genuine intimacy, no friendship and even though I knew it was not healthy, I could not keep away.

We kept in touch, would write letters, and met a couple times of year to be sexual. At this point, we were acting out in sexual addiction and co-sex addition. We were not talking much and sharing ourselves authentically. Bryan shared that he was drinking, doing drugs, and seeing prostitutes on a cyclical basis. Even though there were many red flags, it only intrigued me more. I confused danger and fear with excitement.

A couple of years into my relationship with Bryan, I started to be sexual with other men as a way to fill the emptiness from a lack of emotional connection and from the desperation I felt inside. I rationalized my behavior and went from wanting to be "needless," to acting out to kill the pain and emptiness I felt so deeply inside. I put myself in danger with many encounters of unprotected sex and felt powerless to stop this acting out. At this time, my disease escalated and my boundaries with men broke down completely. There was a driven sexual energy in almost every encounter with a man. For me, there was a consistent longing and a craving for attention. I went to almost any length to receive that attention: dressing provocatively, putting myself in danger of venereal disease, and flirting with married men. There was isolation as well. I did not have close relationships with women as their drive for male attention turned them into competition. I was so obsessive/compulsive in my disease, I often dissociated in my day-to-day life. This was evidenced by the two car accidents I was in that totaled both cars. I self-harmed by cutting myself, drank alcohol to self-medicate and became physically ill for two months.

During this entire time, I felt such yearning and drive to be with Bryan that I felt I might die if he left or I could not be with him. Today, after years of recovery, I know this deep yearning was really about the deep father loss and emotional/spiritual emptiness that I carried inside.

We moved in together after five years of a long distance relationship. When he asked me to do this, I felt victorious on the outside, but in my gut, I was scared. There was still no genuine intimacy and we were strangers in reality. Once we moved in, we did not know how to share ourselves, have fun, or communicate at all. Sexually, the excitement, danger, and uncertainty were gone. The long distance trauma and fantasy had been so key in the relationship. We were now at a loss without it and the emptiness we both felt inside began to surface. Both of us shut down and were unaware of how to connect emotionally. Both of us were exercising and working obsessively as a way to avoid the lack of connection and discomfort we experienced. We relocated together to another city.

While Bryan was out of town, I was unable to function. Driving to the store became frightening. Soon after this, he came home really late one night and I realized that he had been drinking. I was raging and felt out of control. A few days later, I found pornography in our home and confronted him with it. He was shamefully remorseful and promised never to do it again. It happened again and again. Finally, while on line, he found the Sex Addicts Anonymous website and a therapist who specialized in sex addiction. I was stunned by the truth. I had no doubt that addiction was our problem. Soon after, I found out about his full range of acting out behaviors. I started to come out of denial and to attend Co-sex addict meetings.

In Co-Sex Addicts Anonymous, I learned about compulsive behavior and the characteristics of the disease. In therapy and Co-Sex Addicts Anonymous, I realized how low my self-esteem was and how I had used all the acting out I did to try and cover the pain and fill the emptiness inside. I realized that I did not know how to have a healthy relationship and did not understand genuine intimacy. My values were very unclear and I soon began to make connections between how I was set up in my family to be a co-sex addict.

I learned in therapy and in recovery how to align my behaviors with my values and honor what I knew deep inside myself. In working the steps with my sponsor and doing the incident writing in therapy, I slowly began to see clearly how I had made men and my current boyfriend my "higher power." I painfully walked through many episodes of family-of-origin abuse that had me clearly and realistically look at how wounded and dysfunctional my family system really was.

Over time, I am learning to have my feelings of sadness, anger, fear, and shame. I did a lot of shame reduction work by having healthy anger at those who had offended me and holding them accountable rather than blaming myself and continue to feel victimized. I've also done a great deal of grief work, feeling the sadness of what was lost in my childhood and what I was not given and taught.

In recovery, my voice became my own and I was able to set boundaries with those closest to me; trusting my intuition and taking care of myself. Even though this is not always easy, I've learned to reach out to others in recovery and use the tools of the twelve steps to make decisions. There is much that I have had to learn about healthy development. There is a distinction between healthy risks and the attraction of danger and I can feel fear as "fear" rather than as excitement.

Attending Co-Sex Addicts Anonymous meetings is still a part of my week and some of my closest connections and friendships are with sober women committed to living a healthy life in recovery. I have so much gratitude for the clarity I experience and distinctions I have around co-sex and sex addiction. I see how inundated our culture is with this disease and still how charming and seductive it can really be. It is a most precious gift that I am able to feel my authentic joy, recognize healthy fear and have my anger guide me in knowing when my boundaries have been violated and I need to take care of myself.

My boyfriend is now my husband and we have children. In recovery, we have learned to have a healthy and passionate connection. We really enjoy one another and have fun together. We both work our twelve step recovery programs consistently. We seek professional help and assistance from our support systems on a regular basis.

There is much more to share about how the disease affected my educational and professional life and how in recovery I have come to experience transformation in these areas.

While we both know that this is a spiritual journey, we feel grateful for the foundation that we have in our recovery and in allowing our Higher Power to transform our lives. Our relationship continues to deepen and grow. We are emotionally and spiritually available to ourselves, each other, and our children. And as a result, we believe that we are rewriting our family tree.

CHRISTINE'S STORY

As a child I felt invisible, as if I did not matter. It seemed as if no one noticed I was there. But I am here! I was born in a small Midwestern city with a population of about 60,000 in a family with a sister three years older. We lived in a trailer court on the outside of town until I was six. My earliest childhood memories are a little vague.

I recall that my parents would argue a lot and drank excessively. Sometimes my mom would be so drunk she would be passed out on the ground. I went to a few of the bars with her, and the people she was with would want to leave her there. I remember just crying and sobbing when that happened.

I just don't remember my dad being around a lot. He worked nights, and he slept during the day. Sometimes we would have to pick him up at work. I liked that.

I had my sister, but she never really wanted me around much. I was a pain to her a lot, and she would say that to me often. I was in her way. She would just go off with her friends, and I would follow along sometimes.

I was ahead academically in my class and so left to go to another class for reading and felt further alienated from classmates. I remember feeling very lonely and crying often, and even when I did make a friend here and there, my mother would decide ultimately who I could be with and who I could not.

So from about age six to age ten, I remember being very unhappy. My mother was very controlling. It did not seem like I had a lot of contact with the outside world, and if I did have a friend or two, my mother would often yell at me in front of them and embarrass me. When I was six, everything in my life changed when my brother was born. I felt invisible most of the time. But after my brother was born, it seemed like he got all of her attention. And he could do no wrong, absolutely nothing. I stood by and watched him get everything he wanted. I was confused. It seemed as though she was now blaming me for everything, while I watched my little brother get whatever he wanted, whenever he wanted it. I was confused by all of this. During this time, I began to play and excel in sports. I tried to do whatever my mom wanted to keep her from yelling at me and hoping to get her attention and approval. She began working many different odd jobs during this time, and I became responsible for watching my brother often. I did not have many friends, felt lost in the middle of my sister and brother, and felt very sad and lonely a lot.

There was not much affection shared in my family, and I do not recall even being told I was loved. I do recall that on occasion my dad would tuck me into bed at night, and I liked that very much. My father was physically and verbally abusive to my mother, and one time she had to go to the hospital because of a broken finger. He called her names and raged often.

There was a pattern in my life of being alone and not being able to develop friendships outside the family. I also did not feel cared for, nor did I receive attention and parenting from my mother or father, except the negative: yelling, blaming, and neglect.

After I left sixth grade, I went to junior high school. This is where things really started taking a turn for the worse for me. Because of the distance from the school, I was unable to play sports anymore. My dad wasn't around. As long I stayed quiet and didn't say anything, I was okay. I was angry. I was alone. And I was confused. I was in a lot of pain. I even felt at times it would be better if I wasn't around.

This is when I became obsessed with things being in a certain order. I think a lot of that came from my mom. The house had to be spotless. If it wasn't, she would rage about a fork being left in the sink. I started my descent into my addictions in junior high. I started to just not eat (anorexia). I would just starve myself. I didn't really care. And it helped me feel like I had some control over something in my life. It became my entire world. I had good grades. I made sure about that. If I wasn't doing my homework, I was obsessing about food. I had no other outlets. I really don't think I felt anything. I didn't want to feel anything. As long as I thought about the food and not eating, the more I didn't have to feel what was going on around me.

At this time, another piece of my disease came from my father's constant objectifying of women. He had nude women on calendars up in his office, and I would see them day in and day out. A part of me believed that I had to look like that for my dad to notice me, and I knew that I had fallen short of this as well.

My eating disorder became all-encompassing. On the weekends I would eat or pretend to eat, but would also exercise and weigh myself nonstop. This continued into high school and expanded into bulimia and anorexia. I would eat and then vomit and step on the scale any chance I could. I did not think I would be going to college, and sometimes I obsessed about this as well.

In college, the pain continued, as did the bulimia, anorexia, and exercise obsession. I had two roommates my first year. One drank and partied all the time and the other one seemed "normal"—she went to church, had visits from her family, and had a boyfriend. I wanted to be like her. I have known many women in my life that I wanted to be like.

I decided to pursue education and become a teacher. I remember watching my brother's kindergarten class, and I liked being around kids. I thought this was what I wanted to do, but I wasn't really sure since my mom controlled what I did and who I saw.

At a party in college I met a guy named Joe. He was a graduate student, and I was a freshman. He seemed nice enough and gave me some attention. He decided to go to a different college the next year, and I followed him there. My parents were furious, but I did not care. I liked being with him. This was the first of many relationships like this. I saw him when he wanted. He called when he felt like it. I was always waiting for him and available when he finally called.

The bulimia wasn't as bad because I started drinking more. I just found people who wanted to drink every night. I would black out a lot. One Christmas break, John came to pick me up. My mother was raging at me and called me a slut. That night, John assaulted me. He had been kind and not pushy with me up to that point, but this night was horrific. He brought me back home the next day. I just wanted to die.

The rest of that year the bulimia got worse. The summer between my sophomore and junior year, I took myself to the hospital. I got on my bike and went. I knew about this place from when my sister went, and I couldn't stand the bulimia anymore. I knew I couldn't stop. It was so easy to do at school because food was always available. I used to just do it a few times a week or starve myself. But now I was doing it four to five times a day. The psychiatrist on the hospital unit didn't want my parents to have any contact with me. They didn't want me to go back to school. I insisted and went back anyway. I had to promise to get help from doctors at the university hospital, so I did. They put me on antidepressants.

My junior year began, and I continued to meet and date men who used and abused me. On the occasion that I met a kind man, I did not want anything to do with him. I decided to make an attempt on my life by taking all of the antidepressants. My parents didn't even care. They came for one family session, and my dad walked out after he heard about Joe (the one who had assaulted me a year earlier). My psychologist at the time wanted me to tell them about it. And then he thought it was better I had nothing to do with my parents. But that is not what I wanted. I wanted my parents to love me. I felt like a disappointment.

I tried to make my senior year okay. I just knew I wanted to be out of school and on with my life. I worked a lot my senior year. I had a few more boyfriends, but not many. It wasn't like I was going to stay with them anyway. And although I stopped drinking as much, the bulimia was still part of my life.

I got a job teaching, and my parents came for graduation. I was hurting inside. I don't remember much about graduation night because I blacked out. The next morning, my parents drove with me to the city where I would be working but left right away. In fifteen years, I can count on one hand how many times I have seen them since this time.

In the midst of this "drama," I got sober March 17, 1992, and started to go to AA meetings. I got into AA after going to Overeaters Anonymous (OA) for a while. I got sober before I finally quit the eating disorder. I went into a treatment center, and even though it didn't stop the bulimia right away, it did help. I wasn't even going to be accepted into the treatment center because my family wouldn't participate. But a certain therapist did whatever she could to get me into it. My eating disorder was out of control, and I really felt like I was going to die from it. I finally got abstinent on April 25, 1993. I don't think it is any accident that it happened on my brother's birthday.

I found a therapist, and she worked with me for about three years. I was engaged to a guy named William, and it didn't work out either.

He had a lot of porn around, and I insisted he get rid of it. He didn't like the fact that I was in 12-step programs and didn't have a lot of time for him. I ended up getting pregnant. My pregnancy didn't look good to him or his family, so he insisted I have an abortion. That was painful. Afterward, he told me he wished it had never happened and that we hadn't gone through with the abortion. It was too late. He still wanted us to be together. I didn't want anything to do with him. I wanted to talk about it, but he didn't.

While in therapy it started to feel okay to talk about what was bothering me. I just kept picking men who didn't want to communicate. William ended up getting fired from his job and moved.

After two years of abstinence from the eating disorder, I got really depressed and was treated for depression. After I got out of the hospital, I had aftercare. I met this man, Jeffery. I was with him off and on for about five years. I lived with him for a majority of that time. I met him shortly after he was divorced. He was very angry. He didn't like a lot of what I did and the fact that I was in AA and did not drink. My dating and involvement with sex-addicted men who were unavailable and abusive continued. I was in and out of AA, and although it helped me to stay sober, I never quite fit in. I began to work a program about relationships and this helped a bit, but my relationships with unavailable and dishonest men continued. Sometimes I would stay in the relationships because I was so lonely.

I cried out to God to make it better for me. I cried and cried. Nothing was working. I remember going to a Co-Sex Addicts Anonymous meeting the year before, when I was trying to go to different meetings. Then I looked online and called someone I knew who went to them. It was a Friday, July 23, 2005. I have been going to Co-Sex Addicts Anonymous meetings ever since.

It seems like I have been here for a long time. It is the only place in my life where I feel comforted. I got a sponsor pretty quickly. She is wonderful. I don't know where I would be without that. I am learning a lot. I am still making mistakes and learning from them. I have been involved with a few people, but they haven't worked out. But I see it a lot sooner. And the pain doesn't last as long. There is always someone for me to talk to, and I know they are listening when I call. All I have to do is call someone. I have been with sex addicts. It probably wouldn't have mattered if I was married or not. I would have still found my way here. This is where I belong. I feel like I have been this ugly duckling or was made to feel ugly on the inside and have turned out to be a swan . . . that is how it feels to me. I have felt in the past like an orphan, just forgotten about, and that God didn't really care about me at all. That is changing slowly, too. Sometimes I don't want to do this co-sex addiction recovery work. It is hard and painful. I feel like the pain never goes away. When I read this, because I have lived it, it brings a lot of pain to the surface.

I am learning to forgive others and, most of all, myself. I am not giving up on myself, Co-Sex Addicts Anonymous, or God. I do still want to be married one day. I have hope that it will happen. God willing, this relationship won't be like anything I have had in the past.

Nina's Story

Reflecting back on my childhood, I have always thought that I had a pretty good one. I was not physically abused, was well taken care of, always had food on the table, clothes on my back, and my parents were always around. To this day, my parents are still married.

When I started in Co-Sex Addicts Anonymous, I began work on Step 1 and realized that my childhood was less than ideal. I was the second of three girls. My older sister was two years older than me and my younger sister was four years younger than me. I always remember feeling unimportant to my parents. For as long as I can remember, my older sister was my caretaker. I remember that she was always at my side, but I don't remember either of my parents being available to talk with or provide emotional support..

My father had to work two jobs, and my mother was busy trying to keep the house together with three small children. When my dad was around, he was always the "fun" parent. He loved horsing around with us and being the clown. My mother was the disciplinarian for the most part.

By the time I was seven, I realized that my parents were emotionally unavailable. My mother was outwardly resentful and cold. Hugs and affection were rare. My father worked a lot. He was not physically abusive, although he did have angry outbursts from time to time. My mother was very controlling, and my father did not stand up for himself to her. When he did stand up for what he wanted, my mother would get very angry, and he would give in. I guess he thought it was easier to relent than to cause a scene.

Sex was a taboo subject. I never heard a word about it until I was almost an adult. An eight-year-old neighbor told me how babies were made when I was about the same age. I was confused about it, but I did not feel comfortable asking my parents, so I asked the only person I could trust, my older sister. She confirmed that it was true but could not give answers.

I went through puberty at an early age. By age eleven I was fully grown and had breasts and my period. It was a confusing and humiliating time for me. Lots of kids at school made fun of me, and this is when I realized how alone I felt. Boys would chase me around and pop my bra, and girls would chastise me for having breasts and being so tall. Again, I never felt I could go to my parents with any of this. Even my older sister was resentful toward me because I had bigger breasts than she did and started my period about the same time as her.

About this time I started to realize that older boys liked that I had breasts. There were lots of older boys who thought I was much older than I actually was. It made me feel special. One time when my sisters and I had a babysitter, we were playing outside. A neighbor boy who was about fourteen started chasing me around the yard. He ended up chasing me into my house. When inside, he threw me down on the couch and held my hands above my head with one hand, and with the other hand he pulled up my shirt and bra to see my breasts. I just remember being shocked and totally ashamed. I never told anyone about what happened, not even my sister.

When I was twelve I got sick, and my mom decided to take me to a doctor I had never been to before. When the doctor walked into the room, he immediately commented on my age and how developed I was. He made several comments, and I immediately felt uncomfortable. I knew something wasn't right. He proceeded to examine me. When he went to listen to my heart and lungs, he lifted my shirt and bra and stepped back and looked at my breasts. The worst thing about this was that my mother was there and did not say a word, not then or after. I felt so violated, betrayed, unimportant, and unloved.

Beginning high school was exciting, and I immediately had a senior boy interested in going out with me. I ended up losing my virginity to him. I was fourteen years old. I had no idea what I was doing, but I thought I was old enough and needed to get it over with. I thought guys would not like me if I did not do it, so I was too scared to say no. I had several boyfriends in high school, all of whom I had sex with. I was also experimenting with drugs and alcohol.

My senior year I had a boyfriend who my parents loved. I just remember that at last my parents were giving me the attention and love that I had always wanted. They truly trusted me and did not even mind when I would spend the night out with him. I figured out then that I was only as good as the man I was with. As long as I had a good man, I was whole and worthy of love.

College was a blur of drugs, alcohol, and men. I wanted a boyfriend so much, but none of them ever seemed to stick around. I had one-night stands with several men and told myself that it was fun to do that. The reality was that with every man I slept, I felt even more alone and unloved. Many times these encounters with men would lead me to more alcohol and drugs. My life was truly a roller coaster. Throughout all this I managed to do well enough in college to graduate.

My last semester in college, I lived at home. I knew it was time to settle down. I was slowing down with all the men, drugs, and alcohol. I stopped dating for a while and just concentrated on finishing college. It was just about this time when I met Walter at a bar. Within a few dates he told me that he was a sex addict. He said that he was ready to get his life together after many years of struggling with it. I felt special that he had told me. I truly believed that all he needed was a good woman to love and take care of him. We dated for three years with many "slips" on his part, but I still said yes when he asked me to marry him.

I thought he would stop the topless bars and pornography when he was married. I was devastated when only two months into the marriage I found receipts from topless bars. He denied, lied, justified, and so on. This began an eleven-year cycle of him acting out, me catching him, and him either denying it or apologizing and promising never to do it again.

After being married for one year, I thought it would be good to have a baby. A small part of me thought that maybe a child would surely stop his acting out. After a year of trying, we were unable to get pregnant and started fertility treatments. I felt incredibly alone in the whole process, and I knew that when he went to give his sperm samples, there was pornography provided. He lied about not using it, but I knew he was.

Two years of trying to get pregnant with no success was too much for me to handle. Again, I turned to drugs and alcohol to deal with life. During this time I met a woman, and we started an intimate relationship. Walter found out eventually. I truly felt awful about the whole thing and ended it. It was all a rude awakening for me because I knew that it was not me doing those things, and they were not in alignment with my values. To add insult to injury, this gave Walter the ultimate excuse to act out. Every time I caught him, he would tell me how hurt he was about my affair and that is why he acted out.

I stayed in the marriage, and we eventually got pregnant through in vitro fertilization. We had twins, and I remember thinking that Walter would surely not risk losing his family by acting out. One of the defining moments in my life was when I inadvertently found pornography in his car when the twins were only a few months old. That was truly the beginning of the end. I insisted on him going to therapy, which was futile because he intentionally found a therapist who was not knowledgeable about sex addiction. That therapist eventually went on hiatus, and he stopped therapy completely.

When I found out that Walter was having an affair, I was ready to leave the marriage. He begged me to stay. He said that he had never really attempted recovery, and he would really do it this time. He even found a therapist who specialized in sex addiction. He made the appointment, started going to 12-step meetings, the whole nine yards. At this time, his therapist told him about co-addiction. At first I thought there was no way I was a co-addict. I truly thought if he would just stop acting out, our marriage would be happy.

I started attending a 12-step meeting for co-addicts of people involved with sex addicts and began my journey into recovery. I was shocked and relieved because people were saying exactly what I was feeling. I was truly amazed there were women who were in the same situation as mine, and they were happy and doing well in their lives. At this time I also started in therapy that included trauma resolution. I started to realize that this was my problem, that I was a co-sex addict.

About the same time that I started in recovery, I found out that I was pregnant. I was so upset about this. All those years of trying to get pregnant, and I got pregnant out of the blue. What a challenge it was to be pregnant, raise twins, live with a sex addict, and work full-time! It was a difficult time in my life, but I now know that it was a turning point in my life, and I am grateful for that.

My husband's behavior did not change much in recovery. He continued to lie to me and act out. He also picked up a new addiction: gaming. He started obsessing about these games and spending so much money. He was lying to me all the time and constantly on the defensive. I remember one time when we were arguing about his gaming addiction, he told me he was so tired of me being so negative. At the time I beat myself up and told myself that I needed to change my attitude. Now that I look back, it was no wonder that I was so negative!

I gave birth to a little girl and then started formal work on my 12 steps. I felt good about my recovery, but was still struggling with my husband lying all the time. When my daughter was four months old, he confessed to me that he had gone to prostitutes when I was out of town. That is when I knew I could no longer stay in the marriage. I started then to plan my way out. Eight months later, I filed for divorce.

Divorce was drastic, but I could no longer live in the same house with him. He lied to me so often I thought it was detrimental to our children for them to be exposed to that. And what kind of example was I teaching to my daughters to stay with a man who did those things to their mother?

I would love to say that now, one year after my divorce and three years in Co-Sex Addicts Anonymous, everything is wonderful. Sometimes it is, and I still have challenges in my own program and as a single mom. I know more happiness than I have ever known, as long as I stay in recovery. If I have a slip by arguing with my ex-husband or trying to manipulate him, I feel awful. My life is hard, being a single mother of three, but I don't want to change anything. I go to my meetings and do my best to stay in recovery. Without this work, I don't think I would have had the strength to leave my marriage. Without recovery, my life would be empty. In recovery, I am slowly becoming the strong, independent, and loving woman and mother that I have always longed to be.

KATIE'S STORY

Today I know that I am part of intergenerational trauma. Both of my parents came from traumatic childhoods that included alcoholism, neglect, and physical and emotional abandonment, which they carried into their marriage and re-created in our family. My father's father committed my grandmother to a mental institution, and she later committed suicide. She was an alcoholic, and my father carried alcoholism into our family. He also had numerous affairs, which my mother chronicled to me on my wedding night. He was physically and verbally abusive with my brothers and often beat them and got into fistfights regularly. Both of my parents drank heavily on weekends.

My mother's family was part of a big, powerful, politically connected Irish Catholic alcoholic clan and appeared from the outside to be stable and well-established. However, one of the family secrets was that my grandparents married only after their first child was born.

My father was in the military, and we moved twenty-two times in my first eighteen years, never living in more than one place for more than a year until seventh grade. Our housing was always messy with papers stacked everywhere. As a small child, I never actually felt settled. Partly because of this, my mother taught us there is no unit more important than the family. There was nothing one could do to get kicked out of the family. My dad and my brothers tested this in extreme ways, but she endured everything for the "sake of the family." I grew up knowing that a family is an unbreakable unit. That kind of rule requires that one be without boundaries. I never saw my mom set any kind of healthy boundary until I was in my midtwenties, when she divorced my dad.

I am the oldest of four children and was placed in the caretaker role by the family system. My younger brother fell off the changing table at three months old, and this created incredible trauma for my family. We were told that he may not recover and could die in the middle of surgery. If he did survive, doctors told us that he would be retarded. My father valued intelligence above all, especially in men, and now he could have a retarded son. This event defined my family, and even now when traumatic events occur, this event is referenced. I did not seem to be mentioned in this event, and after my mom died, I asked my dad about it. He said that my mother always blamed herself, and when I asked where I might have been when this happened at fifteen months old, he did not know. He thought neighbors may have been taking care of me. I believe this is when I disappeared to my family and became "invisible." My brother, James, did recover but continued to have health problems. There was always a lot of fear around James's survival.

As a child, I was given responsibilities beyond my age. Due to the continued messiness and chaos in our home, I began to clean to try to create order. I worried about getting to school on time and was often late. I was yelled at for losing papers and sometimes stayed up all night dressed, ready for school, to try to cut preparation time in the morning in hopes of being on time. My brother Jack was born around this time, and he, too, was sickly.

My dad, unable to handle all the chaos that surrounded him, went to Vietnam. For me it was a happy and free time, but my brother James remembers my mother being out of control, yelling obscenities, and spanking with the belt.

Fourth grade was also a significant year for me in terms of shame, body image, and fear. I started having my period. I kept my periods a secret, and this was difficult. Very quickly I developed a deep shame about my body. Gynecologists have since told me that this was obviously the result of a hormonal imbalance possibly brought on by stress. Starting my period so early confirmed in my mind that I was "a freak of nature."

The raging, chaos, alcoholism, and physical fighting continued throughout high school. We moved to California for my high school years, and my brothers were acting out in dangerous ways—fistfighting, doing drugs, having sex, stealing cars, and getting arrested. During a fistfight between my father and James, my mother stepped in to stop them. No one noticed at first, and she was hit as hard as they could several times. This was never talked about. The next day we all went about our daily activities—school, homework, and dinner with the family.

I was in the hero role, followed all the rules, and didn't get into trouble. I am brilliant, but I was told to hide my report cards so as to not make my brothers, who were doing badly in school, feel bad. My good grades were not celebrated. It was a secret at home that I earned scholarships to college. My dad also taught me to never let boys know I was smarter than them. That was a bad thing, something to be hidden.

Though I was ignored most of the time, I definitely aimed for invisibility when the drinking, raging, and violence started. That wasn't always possible. Sometimes, when my dad was drunk, he would call me out to the kitchen. He would make me stand there while he told me what was wrong with me. He would start with my face and move down my body. He thought I had an ugly nose, and my ears were uneven. My complexion wasn't pleasant. I had one crooked lower tooth. He thought my breasts were "abnormally small." He made it a point to say that my "abnormally small breasts" couldn't have come from his side of the family—none of the women in his family had such "abnormally small breasts." He didn't like my legs. He thought I had an odd shape. It was unsafe to cross my dad when he was drunk, so I would just stand there and take this in. I don't remember where my mom was on these nights, but she never acted like she knew it happened. I never told her. I just accepted this as further evidence that I was, indeed, a freak of nature. This happened several times, until finally one night I told my dad that I was actually the product of genetics. I had no control over my physical condition. If my appearance bothered him that much, if I was that disgusting, he could pay to have my nose, ears, and breasts surgically corrected. Even though he was drunk, he did not argue, rage, or hit me as I expected. He just listened and said that what I was saying was true. He never criticized my body again. And I never forgot how unpleasant I was to look at.

I couldn't wait to go away to college. Away from my family, I gained confidence, was the social chair of my sorority, and started partying. I met Alex, my husband, during my junior year at a sorority/fraternity party. I remember talking to him at the party, and we were laughing and having a good time. At the same time, I was sizing him up. I distinctly remember thinking that supposedly I'd know right away when I'd met the person I was going to marry. I remember thinking that Alex looked like he'd be fine. How bad could it be? After all, my parents weren't happy in their marriage, but it was really okay. So why spend a lot of time worrying about that? I was nineteen and had known Alex less than an hour, but I was having this conversation with myself in my head.

We started dating after that party. Alex was really fun, funny, smart, and athletic. I thought he was really good-looking. He seemed so normal. And he spent a lot of time with me. No one had ever wanted to spend time with me in my family. We moved so much that

I didn't have much experience with friends. But he sought me out. I felt special. I also thought that, soon, he would come to his senses. He would realize that I wasn't nearly as cool as he was. Within three weeks we were having sex, and although I did not know my own value system at that point, I did know I was acting outside the limitations of my family. We didn't talk at this point about dating each other exclusively. I just assumed it.

When he graduated, he picked up his diploma, his first DUI, and moved to a new city. By this time, I thought that I loved him completely. We talked on the phone every night and spent every break together. After one of these breaks, I found that I had genital warts. I was stunned. I had never had sex with anyone else. How could this have happened? I called him to tell him, because in my disease, I felt responsible. He was my sexual partner, and I had to tell him what diseases I had. I remember thinking that I might have exposed him to this virus—which was insane. When I told him, he immediately told me that he had had those when we were last together, and the reason he had been so depressed was that I hadn't noticed! I hadn't been paying enough attention to him. He had really been depressed about this. For a split second I was stunned again. I know now that this was a *reality switch.** I was being exposed to this disease because of his acting out; he did not tell me about this so that I could choose whether I wanted to have sex with him or not, yet I was being blamed for being insensitive. I knew for just a brief moment that Alex had given these to me. That meant that he had had sex with someone else since we got together. I knew this for the briefest of seconds. Then I put that information away. He probably sent me flowers. We continued the nightly telephone calls, and I continued this pattern of seeing something I couldn't bear to look at for a brief time, feeling shocked and stunned—which is more of a protective reaction than an emotion—and then putting the information out of my mind, going into denial, and carrying on like nothing had happened. This is the first time I remember compartmentalizing.

We continued to have a long-distance relationship, and after three years, Alex asked me to marry him. It was shortly after his second DUI, but I went into denial about this and naively decided that when we married, we would just stop drinking. We would avoid the problems of our parents and have a nurturing, wonderful marriage and family.

Shortly after we married, I realized Alex was drinking again and there was evidence of his sexually acting out. One night I noticed the light on the answering machine was blinking, and when I went to listen to it, a woman named Nikki was inviting Alex to come watch her dance that evening. I was stunned again. Alex took the tape out of the machine and slept in the other room.

The next morning I asked many questions about this woman, and finally Alex said he just went to look, this is what men do, and I would have to get used to this and work on my jealousy and insecurity. It was another reality switch, in which I was made responsible for his acting out. I also slipped back into the belief that I was a "freak of nature" and could hear my father being disgusted with me, noting all my flaws, especially my small breasts. Maybe he just wanted to go and see "normal" large breasts. Again, this is what I've come to learn is a reality switch.

Sometimes he came home with lipstick all over his shirts. He stayed out until 2:00 or 3:00 AM regularly. He would say that the girls were just drunk and sometimes they fell, so there might be lipstick on his shirts, he would never be unfaithful to me, I was just jealous and insecure, and so on.

There were many messages from different women, and the late nights continued. We would argue about the incidents, I would sulk for a few days, and then put it all out of my mind. It never occurred to me to set clear boundaries or to leave Alex. I never told anyone about these problems, nor did I check my reality with anyone other than Alex. Through all this, we continued to try to get pregnant, and I wanted a baby more than anything. After 132 months of failing, I felt more shame.

Alex's job transferred him out of the country, and his alcoholism and acting out escalated. He became very critical of me, and my self-esteem sunk lower. During one weekend overseas, I found a French hooker on my balcony. Another incident occurred when his secretary sat on the other side of him at a company dinner, and I watched them dance, hug, and snuggle the entire evening. I was humiliated. More incidents like this occurred, and my co-sex addiction behavior acting out was to ignore it and try to be a better wife to support him in his career.

Our dreams of having a child were fulfilled in the adoption process. Our son was a tremendous joy. That pure, untainted joy lasted seven weeks. The night he got his two-month shots, he was awake all night screaming. Alex was out all night, and when he came home, I confronted him, telling him I needed help and asking him where he had been. He told me that if I could not handle taking care of a baby to return him to the adoption agency. Then he went to bed. I felt burning hatred and decided I would divorce Alex. If I filed for divorce before the adoption was finalized, we would lose Michael, and so once again, I put my decision to divorce into a compartment where I hid things.

Just before Michael's first birthday, a topless dancer came to our house. Her name was Liza, and she told me that she and Alex had had an eight-year affair. She gave me photos, notes, and receipts. She proved to me that Alex had moved her to Tokyo when we went over there. She told me that she would come to our house in Tokyo every Sunday while I was at church and have sex in my bed.

There were many women after this and incidents of drinking, drugs, and all-night partying. In the fall of 2003, I received a phone call from Alex's cell, and when I answered, no one was talking. Soon I realized his keypad had not been locked and he accidentally called me. I could hear Alex with two other women, doing drugs, having sex, and discussing all the women he had been with recently. I listened for more than an hour before I hung up. I filed for divorce shortly after that, but one day when I picked Michael up at preschool and saw his happy, trusting face, I had a panic attack and called the attorney to stop the paperwork.

I immediately went into a deep depression and finally began to hit bottom. All I can remember is taking care of Michael and nothing else. I found Co-Sex Addicts Anonymous a little more than a year later, which has saved my life.

Doing Step 1 helped me see that I learned the lessons from childhood really well. I learned that I am inadequate and have a lot to be ashamed of. I learned that other people's needs are more important than mine. I learned that a family is an unbreakable unit. I didn't learn any boundaries. About all this I was powerless. I was usually stressed and anxious as a child. I had stress-related physical problems. As an adult, I continued to follow in my mother's footsteps. I learned to ignore information, deny it, and, like my mother, I kept all the alcohol and sex addiction secrets from my friends and family and talked only of pleasant subjects. I also put the incidents of my childhood abuse "away" so completely that I mostly forgot them. They were still hurting my self-esteem and shaming me. But, for the most part, until I started working the steps in Co-Sex Addicts Anonymous, they were gone from my conscious mind. I kept up what looked like, to outsiders, a fun, happy, loving marriage.

As I continued my recovery work, I came to think of my father's treatment of me as an amputation of my self-esteem. As a young child I accepted the role my father gave me: inadequate, ugly, sexually unattractive, awkward. Then, like my parents, I became shame-based.

As a result of intensive therapy and working my Co-Sex Addicts Anonymous program and family of origin work, I now realize that I have kept myself in the role my father assigned. I have maintained it. I have used my husband all these years for that purpose: by cataloging the names, dates, activities, and details of thousands of incidents from his sex addiction for the past eighteen years, my co-sex addict self could be reminded consistently, over time, that I am inadequate, ugly, and sexually "not enough." Even though my denial kept all this information hidden away, I could still access these horrendous experiences enough to keep the amputation of my self-esteem raw and open. I kept that wound open so that I could fulfill the role I was assigned. (Hero children work hard to fulfill their roles. They know their family's survival depends on it.)

My recovery and my life depend on my continuing to do shame work on the carried shame I have from childhood. Today, both my husband and I work our programs and work on our marriage. My recovery and 12-step program also keep me in reality and offer the tools to set boundaries and care for myself in healthy, empowering ways. As I break this cycle of disease that has existed in my family tree, I am able to bring this healing to myself as a woman, mother, partner, sister, and friend. Slowly, I am giving up the intergenerational shame I've been carrying and am embracing healthy self-esteem and sexuality so that I can become the child and the woman God created.

Jo's Story

It was 2:00 AM, and I finally put down the book, *Out of the Shadows*, by Patrick Carnes, Ph.D. It was recommended reading by my "good" therapist, after two years of intense therapy. When I closed the book, I was close to cursing this therapist. *How could she suggest this book to me? I am not a sex addict.* I fell asleep with those thoughts in mind. Three hours later, I woke up and sat straight up in my bed. I was not the sex addict, but the male therapist I had been seeing for eleven years fit that description to a T. I realized that I was the co-sex addict. Having read *Out of the Shadows*, I found myself entering "into the light."

For eleven years I was sexually and emotionally abused by that man. I finally realized that I was co-sexually addicted to him. That began my life-affirming, upward-bound journey toward mental, emotional, and spiritual health. With the help of Co-Sex Addicts Anonymous, I am still on this joyful journey after nearly twenty years. Between the Co-Sex Addicts Anonymous meetings and continued therapy, I began to realize the forces in my life that led me to become a victim of the sex-addicted therapist who called his group members "his family" and then emotionally damaged us by his sexual abuse. Having sex with a family member, as he referred to us, is incest.

Why was I so susceptible to this abusive person? I was often hit and verbally abused by both of my parents. My sister tells me of times when I was slapped or punched by my father. I know my mother raged and hit me many times. My sister and I were abused both emotionally and physically. We had two parents who raged and cursed at us whenever something went wrong. During my mother's raging, she yelled horrible things at us that were sexually inappropriate and very shaming. My father also said things that were sexually inappropriate and made me cringe at times. I believe that this was also sexual abuse. My sister and I lived in fear of both parents. She hid in closets, and I hid in books. Learning to give the shame back to my parents, and feeling the pain that I had stuffed, has been part of my path to recovery. Practicing forgiveness toward myself and others has been a significant part of my recovery process.

I realized that I acted out my pain sexually. My extreme codependence on men in my life, especially my first husband and my sexually addicted male therapist, led me to the Co-Sex Addicts Anonymous recovery program. Admitting my own addictive behavior and learning how harmful it was to me, my children, and the people I cared for was the first step. I looked at my life and saw how lonely I had been for most of it. There were lots of sexually addicted, abusive men in my life, and I grew up surrounded by family, but I had no sisters of the soul or truly intimate partners. This black hole of loneliness was a wound in my heart. I acted out to fill that hole.

Our Co-Sex Addicts Anonymous program is a healing program, and the promises we hear at every meeting do come true. God shed his light on new and wonderful paths for me. First and foremost, I found my spirituality. I began a relationship with God, who is my Higher Power. The program has brought many loving women into my life, women with whom I have shared my most intimate secrets and who still love me in their special way. When I was ready, God gave me the enlightenment that not all men are evil or hurtful. Those kinds of men can be avoided when I walk a different path. My present partner is my loving husband. He is a caring person who shares my spiritual path and experiences both the joys and pains of life with me.

My co-sex addiction and the sex addict therapist had stymied my professional life. After several years in the program, I went back to school, graduated just short of my fiftieth birthday, and have had a successful practice for many years. Today I am no longer a lonely young girl looking through a window at "perfect" families in their "perfect" homes. I enjoy an abundance of real friends, both in and out of the program. The black hole of loneliness is gone. Of course, I experience many pains and losses. Three years ago I was diagnosed with ovarian cancer. At first I was terrified to the point of numbness. One more time, however, my spirituality, my trust in a loving God, and my Co-Sex Addicts Anonymous program got me through. I remember one warm September afternoon, resting and recuperating from chemo, thinking that I was a most blessed person. I felt the joy of God's love for me as expressed through the love and caring of so many dear people. My husband was at my side through it all, and my son called every day. Friends and medical caretakers blessed me with smiles and hugs I will never forget. My Co-Sex Addicts Anonymous sisters called me, prayed with me, and even brought a meeting to my house when I needed one most but could not get there.

Few of us go through life without similar painful experiences. I weep today for broken relationships and daily hurts. But feeling the pain, working the program, and trusting my Higher Power allow me also to feel the joy as promised by our Co-Sex Addicts Anonymous program.

In Closing

There are so many blessings that we have experienced both as individuals on our journeys of recovery and as coauthors of this book. It is an honor to both witness and be witnessed in the healing journey. We thank all of the individuals who have had the courage to share with us their stories, both before and after the miracles of working the program.

To all who still suffer, you are not alone, and we invite you to create the life you desire with relationships based in powerful serenity and authentic connections with yourself and others. It doesn't happen overnight, but it does happen. There are communities available to you to assist in the transformation. We believe when the student is ready, the teacher will appear, as will the courage, the willingness, the support, and everything else that is necessary for the healing to happen.

Last, we encourage you to trust the process, the program, your own individual spiritual source, and the synchronicities that begin to occur in your life, and eventually you will find a deep and lasting authentic trust in yourself.

We look forward to hearing from you and sharing in the miracles of recovery.

Blessings on your journey,

Sally and Claudine

Appendix:
Co-Sex Addiction
Resource Guide

*I*n this Appendix, we offer a Co-Sex Addiction Resource Guide, which has been copyrighted and used in various circles for several years now. This is something that we give permission to use as a quick resource for identifying co-sex addiction and relationship addiction that may be present to varying degrees. We also offer tools and practices that we have found effective in addressing individual and relationship issues of all kinds. This Appendix may be copied and used for the purpose of education and recovery from co-sex addiction in a nonprofit and recovery setting.

WHAT IS CO-SEX ADDICTION?

Over time, we of Co-Sex Addicts Anonymous have gained awareness of our disease and have begun the road to recovery and healing. Most of us come to our first meeting on the recommendation of a therapist or friend. We are willing to take that step because we are in pain over a relationship with a sex addict and what we see as his problem. Over time, we come to realize we too have a disease. The addictive behaviors associated with this disease affect every area of our lives. Initially, we recognize that the enmeshment with the sex addict has been our primary focus. As we practice the principles of the program, we begin to take responsibility for the disease we have and how it affects all areas of our lives.

In attending meetings and working our spiritual program of recovery, we learn that co-sex addiction has devastating consequences for our emotional, physical, financial, sexual, and spiritual well-being. Symptoms of the disease show up in our obvious relationships with the sex addicts close to us and/or in our less obvious relationships and encounters with others.

Part of this disease is focusing too much on the sex addict's behavior and minimizing the seriousness of our co-sex addiction. We often have difficulty staying out of denial about our disease and that of the sex addicts in our lives. We spend much time and energy covering up or keeping secret the addict's acting out or our own acting out. Oftentimes, we may not have physical evidence of the addict's sexual acting out, and we live with uneasiness or an intuitive gut sense that something is wrong and something is going on. In our disease, however, we do not trust our own intuition or sense of uneasiness, and we live with many symptoms of the disease without knowing it. When we are overly focused on others' feelings and needs, it takes time to separate and recognize our own thoughts, feelings, and needs. As we work the program of co-sex addiction recovery, we gain our own reality and learn to trust ourselves.

Another aspect of co-sex addiction is trying to control or fix the addict's feelings and attempting to alter his behavior. This comes from a sense of over-responsibility and deep sense of emptiness developed long ago in our own childhood experiences. We may have been set up at a very young age to feel responsible for others' feelings and behaviors and to actually carry the shame of an offender's behavior or reality. This dynamic may have occurred as a result of overt sexual, physical, emotional, and/or verbal abuse. It may also have occurred as a result of more covert dysfunctional family behaviors such as neglect, absence, over-responsibility, unresolved family trauma, perfectionism, or shaming. Being set up when young to be a victim of another's behaviors, feelings, thoughts, and actions is the foundation of our disease.

Another, more major characteristic of co-sex addiction is thinking and really believing that if we were only prettier, thinner, smarter, stronger, less needy, and so on, the addict or addicts in our lives would not act out or behave as they do. Taking responsibility for another's choices and behaviors, as well as being made to feel guilty or wrong for our feelings and needs related to the relationship, is common in our disease.

Learning to recognize our disease for what it is, accepting our powerlessness over the disease, and transforming our victim behavior to empowered behavior is the journey of recovery from co-sex addiction. One thing we are able to assure all interested in changing their lives and living differently is that there is hope and healing. This 12-step program guides us out of the darkness and hopelessness of the disease into the light and freedom of healing and recovery.

SYMPTOMS AND BEHAVIORS OF CO-SEX ADDICTION DISEASE

One, some, or all of these behaviors may apply:

- Basing our feelings of value/worth on others' opinions of us
- Tolerating verbal, physical, sexual, emotional, or financial abuse
- Choosing clothing to provoke sexual attention or dressing very sloppily to deflect sexual attention
- Getting a high from dressing provocatively
- Believing that our value is primarily connected to our physical/sexual appearance
- Dressing or behaving to please others when it is uncomfortable for us or against our individual value system
- Thinking that there is not enough (lack mentality)—we are not enough, we cannot generate enough income for ourselves, there are not enough men, not enough time, we are not pretty enough, smart enough, and so on
- Being drawn to dysfunctional people and/or situations (high drama, chaos, and intensity generated by people who turn out to be deceptive and abusive)

- Constantly comparing ourselves to others and judging ourselves or others (lack mentality)

- Feeling superior or inferior to others (grandiosity, lack mentality/shame)

- Feeling afraid of and threatened by others, particularly the "competition"

- Feeling that the world is full of enemies and unfair, thus generating isolation and self-protectiveness, fear of intimacy

- Feeling victimized, being easily taken advantage of by others

- Fear of being sexual and fear of one's own sexuality and others' sexuality

- Being sexual with others to please them or gain their approval or outside of our own value systems

- Not being able to say no when appropriate or to say yes when we really want to

- Fantasizing about relationships

- Wanting to be rescued by a relationship or being the rescuer in a relationship

- Confusing sex with love and love with sex

- Using sexuality to reward or punish another

- Risking physical/emotional safety for a relationship—for example, putting oneself at risk for sexually transmitted diseases

- Neglecting our own hobbies, interests, and social circles, and spending our time sharing another's interests and hobbies

- Being unaware of how we feel, what we need, think, and want, and being overly focused on how others feel, need, think, and want

- Putting aside our own values for the sake of the relationship and valuing others' opinions and ways of doing things more than our own

- Feeling responsible for another's happiness and losing sight of our own happiness, passions, and desires

SYMPTOMS AND BEHAVIORS OF
CO-SEX/SEX-ADDICTED RELATIONSHIPS

One, some, or more of these behaviors in a relationship may apply. A co-sex addict in a relationship with a sex addict may:

- Have a pattern of raging, threatening to leave, and then staying over and over again

- Have a strong, persistent anxiety about the partner and the relationship

- Constantly feel threatened in situations where other people are present

- Frequently check for signs that the partner is acting out—by snooping, spying, checking pockets for evidence, reviewing Internet activity, and so on

- Believe that she can control the addiction by throwing away pornography, changing her own appearance/behavior, catering to sexual demands

- Look for attention/validation outside of the relationship, sometimes in a sexual manner

- Become obsessively busy, involved with external activities such over-volunteering, workaholism, and so on

- Blame herself for her partner's addiction and blame her partner for her unhappiness/addiction

- Create chaos, crisis, and drama to distract from the pain/addiction in the relationship

- Use sex to smooth over arguments, fix troubles, and make the addict feel better

- Protect the addict and/or cover up the addict's behavior to family, friends, and society
- Rationalize/minimize the addict's or her own addictive behavior

RELAPSE PREVENTION TOOLS— OUR EXPERIENCE, STRENGTH, HOPE, AND HEALING

There is hope for the co-sex addict seeking a new way of living. Some of the tools and techniques we use in seeking healing and recovery include:

Attending Meetings Regularly

Attending meetings regularly allows us the honor of listening to recovering Co-Sex Addicts Anonymous members and learning from the experience of those who have gone before us. Meetings are also a sacred space for speaking our truth, expressing our feelings, and seeking feedback from appropriate people after the meeting has ended.

Application of the 12 Steps of Co-Sex Addicts Anonymous

When we begin to formally write our personal 12 steps of recovery, we begin to break free from the shame, fear, and pain of secrecy from living in addiction. Formally writing out our steps and sharing with an experienced Co-Sex Addicts Anonymous sponsor is a powerful tool for releasing the pain that we carry and beginning to live more spontaneously and authentically. Eventually, we internalize the wisdom of each of the 12 steps and use them in our lives on a daily basis.

Sponsorship

Sponsorship* is a significant and powerful source of recovery. Newcomers are encouraged to find a sponsor within their first thirty days into the program. It is recommended that a sponsor be someone who is actively attending meetings each week, has her own more experienced sponsor in Co-Sex Addicts

Anonymous, and has formally worked the 12 steps. A sponsor is chosen by each individual Co-Sex Addicts Anonymous member and is generally someone who you have an attraction to know, who demonstrates for you behaviors that you want for yourself, and who is available and able to guide you through working your formal 12 steps. Asking people if they are available to sponsor is the best way to begin that relationship.

Reading Co-Sex Addicts Anonymous Literature

Reading Co-Sex Addicts Anonymous literature is a good source of inspiration, information, and knowledge about this disease. Learning the symptoms, family dynamics, and behaviors associated with co-sex addiction and sex addiction assist all of us, especially newcomers, in understanding and taking responsibility for recovery from this disease.

Phone Support

Phone support is one of the foundations of the program for many Co-Sex Addicts. Knowing that we have support, nurturing, and wisdom outside of meetings provides us the necessary encouragement to make it through those difficult moments and challenges in our family and friendship relationships. In meetings, there are notebooks with names and numbers of members who are willing to be called. Co-Sex Addicts Anonymous members are encouraged to use this valuable resource.

Setting Boundaries

As we grow in the program, we learn more and more about our own individual needs and wants, and how to care for ourselves. Setting boundaries with ourselves and others is an important self-care and relationship behavior that we use. Setting boundaries relates to knowing when to say no and when to say y^r
Learning to attend to our own physical and spiritual needs and desires i^s
of working the program and doing our own individual recovery worl

Detachment

Detachment is another behavior that we learn from a co-sex addiction recovery program. Knowing how and when to detach is a learned behavior that we progress in over time. In detaching with love and compassion, we learn to separate our emotional and spiritual energy from the other addict(s) in our lives. This emotional separation is what allows each person the clarity and wisdom to deal effectively with an addictive dynamic. Detachment is especially necessary for the recovering co-sex addict, as part of the disease is a tendency toward enmeshment and weak boundaries.

Journaling

Journaling refers to the use of writing as a tool for self-awareness and self-knowledge. Oftentimes, journaling is the only way for us to recognize the source of emotional pain and clarity about what is driving our behavior. Used on a regular basis, journaling becomes a powerful resource for insights and guidance in our recovery process.

Prayer and Meditation

Co-sex addiction recovery is a spiritual program. Prayer and meditation are essential tools in this journey. There are several 12-step prayers that can be used, daily meditation books to read, and individual methods to develop our prayer and meditation practices. Taking a daily inventory is a helpful tool, and some sponsors encourage this practice. How we define our Higher Power is an individual choice. In the program, we have the freedom to honor our own internal beliefs and values. For many co-sex addicts, verbally saying the first three steps every morning is a great practice for their spiritual prayer and meditation. Also, saying the *Co-Sex Addicts Anonymous Prayer** is another powerful tool we use.

Developing Our Relationship with Our Higher Power

Many of us come to Co-Sex Addicts Anonymous with some type of religious or spiritual experience in our backgrounds. In the program, the development of this relationship, characteristics, and beliefs around a Higher Power is individualized and may vary widely. Some Co-Sex Addicts Anonymous members choose to re-create their Higher Power based on their unique beliefs and values. Some no longer practice the religious traditions handed down to them. In other situations, the religious and spiritual beliefs handed down are embraced and deepened through their experiences in recovery.

Sharing in Co-Sex Addicts Anonymous Meetings and Listening to Others

Attending meetings in recovery is invaluable. At first we may be too shocked, scared, or overwhelmed with pain to speak during the meetings or afterward. In time, we learn that walking through the fear and discomfort of speaking at meetings has a great value of its own. When we hear ourselves speak, break the silence, and risk reaching out, we feel connected to others, and the road to recovery is expedited. There are also times when listening is the best thing that we can do for our recovery.

Turning It Over and Living One Day at a Time

There are many slogans in recovery that become a part of our daily lives. As we begin to experience more and more serenity and peace in our lives, our commitment to living in recovery increases. In those moments when we attempt to control, manipulate, or obsess about someone else's or our own behavior, we utilize the tool of turning it over and trusting all people, places, and things into the hands of a Higher Power. This Higher Power is individualized for each person.

Living "one day at a time" means learning to live in the present, not the past or the future. Because we cannot change the past or determine or predict the future, it is in the present moment, living one day at a time, that we can influence our relationships with ourselves and others. As we use the tools of the program, we grow and learn how to live authentically. Reclaiming our ability to identify our feelings, release those feelings, and heal from past hurts is the essence of our recovery.

12 STEPS OF CO-SEX ADDICTS ANONYMOUS

1. Admitted we were powerless over our co-sex addiction disease and others' sex addiction and that our lives had become unmanageable.

2. Came to believe in a Power greater than ourselves that could restore us to sanity.

3. Made a decision to turn our will and our lives over to the care of this Power as we understand it.

4. Made a searching and fearless moral inventory of ourselves.

5. Admitted to ourselves, our Higher Power, and another human being the exact nature of our wrongs.

6. Became entirely ready to have our Higher Power remove all these defects of character.

7. Humbly asked our Higher Power to remove our shortcomings.

8. Made a list of all people we had harmed and became willing to make amends to them all.

9. Made direct amends to such people whenever possible except when to do so would injure them or others.

10. Continue to take personal inventory, and when we are wrong promptly admit it.

11. Sought through prayer and meditation to improve our conscious contact with our Higher Power, praying only for the knowledge of

our Higher Power's will and the courage to carry it out.

12. Having had a spiritual awakening as a result of these steps, we carried this message to others and practiced these principles in all areas of our lives.

Co-Sex Addicts Anonymous gratefully acknowledges Alcoholics Anonymous for the AA 12 Steps from which our Co-Sex Addicts Anonymous 12 Steps were created.

12 PROMISES OF CO-SEX ADDICTS ANONYMOUS

We know from our own commitment to recover and our experience in using these tools that our lives will be transformed. We will begin to experience these promises and see these miracles come true. Having had a spiritual awakening as a result of working our Co-Sex Addicts Anonymous 12-step program:

1. We will know a new freedom and experience joyful living.

2. We will fully embrace our past, and see how wisdom and maturity grew out of our pain and addictive behavior.

3. We will know peace, serenity, and a genuine connection to ourselves and others.

4. We will share our experience to make a difference in the lives of others.

5. Our lives will be purposeful, and we will grow in self-esteem and self-appreciation.

6. We will gain a healthy interest in our own lives and give to others from a place of fullness within.

7. Our whole attitude and outlook on life will change.

8. We will welcome prosperity in all areas of our lives.

9. We will grow to trust ourselves and learn how to choose trustworthy people.

10. A healthy sense of fear will guide us in unsafe situations, and our self-confidence will grow.

11. We will intuitively know how to handle situations that once baffled us.

12. We will suddenly realize that our Higher Power is doing for us what we could not do for ourselves.

Co-Sex Addicts Anonymous gratefully acknowledges Alcoholics Anonymous for the AA Promises upon which our Co-Sex Addicts Anonymous Promises were created.

BEHAVIORS OF CO-SEX ADDICTS ANONYMOUS RECOVERY IN RELATIONSHIPS

As we begin to experience these changes in our own lives, we will begin to see transformation in our relationships as well. This includes our marriage, committed partnerships, family relationships, and friendships.

Co-sex addicts in recovery have discovered that the quality of their relationships will continue to improve. Progress in the areas of intimacy, trust, and commitment will occur over time. Here are other specific ways we see progress toward more intimate and healthy relationships:

• We experience serene and peaceful coexistence.

• Authentic joy and genuine laughter increase.

• The ability to be together and enjoy one another's company increases.

• The ability to be apart and enjoy our own company also increases.

• We are fully empowered to choose to be sexual or not to be sexual.

• We are guided by our authentic intuition, and ongoing guidance from our Higher Power becomes a part of our relationships.

- We develop healthy boundaries with others and ourselves.

- We become able to resolve conflict effectively and to negotiate issues with others.

- Trust and intimacy in our relationships grow over time.

- A commitment to each other's and the relationship's highest good replaces self-centeredness and blame in the relationship.

- We become more emotionally available and present to ourselves and one another. With the guidance of a Higher Power and other recovering co-sex addicts, we learn together to change our thinking and alter our behavior to reflect that of mature, strong, and spiritual beings. Our 12-step meetings become a safe place to share our feelings, realities, challenges, and victories.

Working the steps and attending meetings regularly allow us to access our feelings. In doing so, we are able to feel and release the feelings we have in the present and grieve those unresolved from the past. Through this process, we become more fully present and available to ourselves and those we love. We also know from our experience in working the program that our abuse histories and individual journeys vary greatly. We can, however, assure even the most hopeless and seemingly lost co-sex addicts that healing and growth will occur, one day at a time, using the tools and techniques of this recovery program.

Eventually, we find ourselves able to reach out to others in need from a place of fullness within and welcome health, serenity, and integrity into all areas of our lives.

12-Step Guide for Co-Sex Addicts Anonymous Step Writing

There are many paths to formally working the 12 steps with a sponsor, and each COSA member and sponsor is free to individualize her process.

These are suggested formats for doing step work in Co-Sex Anonymous:

Step 1: Admitted we were powerless over our co-sex addiction disease and others' sex addiction and that our lives had become unmanageable.

Writing an autobiography beginning with our earliest memory is a powerful first-step format. As we begin to write the memories that make up our stories, we can begin to see how we were set up in a system to act as a co-sex addict. Reading this to a sponsor and specifically writing all the ways that we were powerless breaks the denial and provides a perspective of reality. This also provides insight and information to the sponsor. List ways your life was/is unmanageable. Sometimes using a different color pen to distinguish between powerlessness and unmanageability is useful.

Step 2: Came to believe in a Power greater than ourselves that could restore us to sanity.

Here we begin to look honestly at our present relationship with our Higher Power or lack thereof.

- Write the characteristics that you currently attribute to your Higher Power/God.

- Make a list of characteristics of your mother, father, and/or other primary caregivers in your childhood.

- Pay attention to how different or similar the lists may be. Write your thoughts and feelings about the lists.

- Write down all the ways that you currently connect with your Higher Power/God/spirituality.

- Now make a final list of all the characteristics from the list you have that you *choose* to have as your Higher Power. Draw from your existing list and add characteristics that you want to be there that may be missing.

Step 3: Made a decision to turn our will and our lives over to the care of this Power as we understand it.

- Recalling insights from Steps 1 and 2, write a letter to your Higher Power. In the letter, thank your Higher Power for getting you to this place. In it, also release current areas of unmanageability and powerlessness in your life.

- Keeping all areas of unmanageability and powerlessness from your life in mind, include in the letter that you now make a decision to turn your will and life over to your Higher Power as you understand it today. Complete the letter, however it feels right to do so.

Step 4: Made a searching and fearless moral inventory of ourselves.

- List all your positive characteristics.

- On another sheet of paper, list all of your harmful behaviors and/or negative characteristics. Pay special attention to how you were set up and continue to set yourself up as a victim. Being a victim shows up in our relationships, financial areas, health, and physical arena, and with our children and family relationships, sexuality, and so on.

This is an important step in recognizing and owning our existing resentments and anger at others and ourselves. Seeing our part in these areas does not mean that we excuse others' abusive behaviors. It does mean that we honestly look at how we allowed ourselves to be victims in these situations, listing those specific shortcomings that we identified.

Step 5: Admitted to ourselves, our Higher Power, and another human being [sponsor] the exact nature of our wrongs.

This is a groundbreaking step in recovery. Looking honestly at ourselves, family systems, and our victim behavior and then sharing with another human being begins to break the pattern of addictive behavior. It also

provides us the opportunity to share with our sponsor and receive uncondi-
tional acceptance and love, and it begins to diminish the shame we've been
carrying. It is especially important to share honestly with our sponsor what
we perceive as our part, since co-sex addicts tend to confuse their own feelings, behaviors, and responsibility with others.

Step 6: Became entirely ready to have our Higher Power remove all these defects of character.

There are several suggestions for doing the sixth step. Some think of this
step as a meditation step, not a "doing" step. Others think it is an important
time to write and/or do ritual. Here are some suggestions:

- Meditate on what you have learned so far, praying for willingness, if
  necessary; or simply ask your Higher Power to help you become ready.

- Draw a large circle on a piece of paper. Write the character defect on the outside
  of the circle. Find the positive that came from that shortcoming or harmful
  behavior. For example, if one of your character defects is judging others, perhaps
  the positive could be your recognizing it as a reflection of you and developing
  increased self-awareness. Another example: if you are attracted to unsafe people,
  perhaps the positive could be recognizing this and using your intuition to take
  care of yourself.

- Cut out the circle and burn or discard the outside. Place the inner
  circle somewhere in your home.

- Ask God to remove victim behavior from you. List the defects again
  and list the behaviors with which you would like to replace the victim
  behavior.

Step 7: Humbly asked our Higher Power to remove our shortcomings.

Pay special attention to your willingness or lack of willingness in regard to
having these defects of character and/or addictive behaviors removed. It may

be appropriate to list where you feel unwilling to let go and ask yourself, "What am I afraid will occur if I really let go?" Share any insights with your sponsor and continue to pray for courage and willingness.

Say the Step 7 prayer daily: "Creator, I am now willing that you should have all of me, good and bad. I pray now that you remove my co-sex addiction character defects that stand in the way of my usefulness to you. Grant me strength and courage to be open to your will. Amen."

Step 8: Made a list of all people we had harmed and became willing to make amends to them all.

The most important way to make amends to ourselves and to others is by changing our behaviors one day at a time.

Reread your first and fourth step work. We put ourselves at the top of the list as a powerful affirmation of recognizing how we have been wounded. By doing so, we begin to reclaim our power and affirm our value. We also list all others we have hurt by our behavior and pray for willingness and guidance.

Step 9: Made direct amends to such people whenever possible except when to do so would injure them or others.

With the guidance of our Higher Power and sponsor, we also make direct amends to others when appropriate. This may include a letter written to them, a verbal communication, meeting face-to-face, or whatever you determine is appropriate. Making amends to ourselves means changing the ways we treat ourselves and developing new practices in our daily lives.

Here are some suggestions for self-amends:

• Attending meetings and other nurturing support groups

• Exercising and healthful practices

• Practicing daily prayer and meditation

• Choosing only kind, healthy, and respectful people with whom to be in relationships

- Following your dreams and passions

Now add your own self-amend ideas . . .

Step 10: Continue to take personal inventory, and when we are wrong promptly admit it.

As we grow and progress in our recovery, we will gain clarity around when and how to make amends appropriately. Many recovering co-sex addicts do an evening inventory before bed. This practice can be written or not. It is always appropriate to get feedback from our sponsor and other recovering co-sex addicts when we have questions about our part and when or how to make amends.

Co-sex addicts especially need this guidance, as part of the disease is to be victimized and to then carry the feelings/shame for the other's behavior. When we carry the shame for another's behavior, we tend to make amends and act over-responsibly, rather than confronting the offensive behavior and setting our boundaries to care for ourselves.

Step 11: Sought through prayer and meditation to improve our conscious contact with our Higher Power, praying only for the knowledge of our Higher Power's will and the courage to carry it out.

Prayer is about asking for guidance and expressing gratitude, while meditation is about learning to be open and receive guidance from our Higher Power.

Other ways to improve our conscious contact with our Higher Power include:

- attending Co-Sex Addicts Anonymous meetings regularly
- practicing the principles of the 12 steps in our lives
- reading the Co-Sex Addicts Anonymous 12 steps prayer daily
- developing a practice of morning and evening meditation

• saying the first three steps every day

Now add your own ways . . .

Step 12: Having had a spiritual awakening as a result of these steps, we carried this message to others and practiced these principles in all areas of our lives.

Now is the time to integrate the 12 steps into our lives. Sponsoring other co-sex addicts and guiding them through their 12-step writing is a powerful contribution and service. Being open to our Higher Power's guidance on a regular basis allows us to share with others who are in pain and looking for healing in their lives. Chairing meetings, leading meetings, and doing service work in the organization are also powerful ways to share our recovery and be of service to others.

∼ CO-SEX ADDICTS ANONYMOUS ∼
12-STEP PRAYER

I come to you today, my Higher Power, because my life has become unmanageable and I am powerless. I believe in Your Power to restore me to sanity and to show me the way in co-sex addiction recovery. Since my choices in my disease of co-sex addiction have been ineffective, I have decided to turn over my life and will to Your Power. I give You all of me—my will, my thoughts, my desires, and my wishes. These things are in Your Power, and I seek to know Your Plan.

I cannot change or control my loved ones, friends, or enemies. So I give You my control issues and judgments. I place these in Your care. If others need changing, You must do it—I cannot. I can only change myself with the help of Your Power.

Help me see how my co-sex addiction behavior has harmed myself and others. As I take my co-sex addiction inventory, help me not forget my goodness.

Lead me through the fifth step of Co-Sex Addicts Anonymous, to share with myself, my sponsor, and with You, my Higher Power, the exact nature of my wrongs, not forgetting my goodness.

May I be entirely ready to have You, my Higher Power, remove my defects of character, and I ask You to remove my shortcomings.

Help me make a list of all those I have harmed, not forgetting that I belong on the list. May You recognize my willingness to make amends. Show me the way to carry that out and to know when doing so might damage others.

I will make direct amends when appropriate.

When my actions separate me from Your Light and Love, return me to these principles through Co-Sex Addicts Anonymous meetings, the 12 steps, and the guidance of my sponsor. These things help me do the right thing.

Remind me that daily meditation and prayer are my link to growth and may I practice these things to keep me in constant contact with You, my Higher Power.

Having had a spiritual awakening as a result of these 12 steps of Co-Sex Addicts Anonymous, may I carry this message to other co-sex addicts and practice the Co-Sex Addicts Anonymous principles in all areas of my life. Amen.

Inspired by the *12-Step Prayer of AA and AlAnon.*

Glossary

abusers/offenders: those who have hurt or wronged us; those who strike against us with any transgression of law, human or divine. May include verbal, physical, sexual, spiritual, or intellectual abuse, or violation of us in any form.

acting out: behavior that we follow in our disease.

addiction: the act of giving up oneself to a habit.

addictive cycle: the habitual repetition of the dynamic between the co-sex addict and the sex addict. It begins with the obsessive thoughts of acting out followed by the acting out, then the remorse and the determination to not act out again (for the co-sex addict, snooping, wanting to fix situations with sex, etc., and for the sex addict, getting the fix by sexually acting out, phone sex, Internet porn, etc.). As the tension builds, the cycle repeats itself and continues over and over unless intervention occurs.

assigned patient: this child is often ill with allergies and is sickly, as well as fearful of contracting all sicknesses.

assigned roles: the roles that were "assigned" to us in our family of origin that, without intervention and recovery, we will automatically revert to in our disease. For the co-sex addict, this is primarily being identified in the "victim role," and with the sex addict, it is primarily being identified in the "offender role."

authentic intimacy: the ability to be fully present in our relationships. It includes having and expressing our feelings and having healthy boundaries, including saying yes when we mean it and saying no when we mean it. In a relationship characterized by authentic intimacy, both parties have the freedom to take care of themselves sexually and emotionally inside the relationship and care for each other in supportive, mature ways.

authentic reality: refers to the ability to see and live in the actual occurrences within the relationship; seeing the facts and truthful realization of the dysfunctional and addictive dynamics taking place.

automatic behaviors: any action without plan or forethought.

Big Offender and little victim: his main role is offender, but he can be a victim. It is the dynamic that occurs when an offender is offended. Example: He sexually abused his wife, but two days later she victimized him and he became the little victim when she says "his sexual organ is too small."

Big Victim and little offender: the co-sex addict is raped by her partner, becoming the Big Victim. She then uses the rage she didn't share with her offender to beat her children, thus becoming a little offender.

carried shame: is about something that happened "to you" for which you carry the feelings of shame for the offender(s) that abused you. For example, it is common for incest survivors to be shame-based from the internal belief that something is wrong with them; thus, they carry the shame of the sex addicts who abused them.

Co-Sex Addicts Anonymous prayer: an adaptation for co-sex addicts of the 12-step prayer, which is an anonymous prayer considering the 12 steps of AA and AlAnon.

co-sex addiction: the act of giving up oneself for another human being, especially someone addicted to sex.

denial: the behavior that occurs when an individual consistently denies what she knows, she sees, hears, and/or intuitively experiences regarding the addict's behavior. This sets up the individual as easy prey to the "reality switch" of an addicted dynamic. The *payoff** for the co-sex addict is that she can remain in denial about what is really going on in the relationship(s) and does not have to take action or deal with her own fears of abandonment or conflict. The payoff for the addict is that he continues to be free to act out and get his fix in the disease.

depression: within the context of co-sex and sex addiction, we refer to depression as the natural outcome of holding feelings inside one's body. When anger, fear, sadness, and/or other emotions are turned inward and not expressed, the result is often depression. This may include a lack of energy, focus, serenity, and the ability to authentically connect with others. We also believe that sometimes there is a chemical imbalance as the source of depression that needs to be addressed as well.

emotional abuse: a common occurrence in dysfunctional systems. It occurs when one or both parents use children to attempt to fulfill emotional wants and needs for themselves. These roles should be filled by parents, peers, and functional, healthy adult support systems, not by their children.

emotional affair: the act by which individuals connect in an emotional way, sharing intimate information that is normally reserved for a partner and/or marriage relationship. This emotional connection often occurs in secret. This emotional connection also occurs within the context of there being no opportunity for commitment on the part of both or one of the individuals, that is, married people at work, priests, authority figures, online chatting, and so on. Sometimes the rationalization for an emotional affair is that there is no sexual contact and not enough of what we need in our partnerships or in other areas of our lives.

emotional incest: when a person of power uses that power to get needs and wants met emotionally in a relationship with someone of less power. This is without regard for the other individual's spiritual, emotional, or psychological needs. The person of power's primary objective is emotional gratification. This occurs when the adults in a family "use" their children for emotional support and/or sharing private, personal, and adult information with them.

empowerment: accepting one's innate power and acting from it.

enable: to permit another to be offensive and/or protecting another from the natural consequences of their choices and behaviors.

enabler: one who allows abuse.

enabling behaviors: behaviors in our co-sex addiction disease that lead us into denial, fixing, minimizing, and/or covering up the addict's behavior. These *enabling behaviors* keep the addict from "hitting bottom" and facing his addiction and the consequences of his disease.

enculturation: defined in *Encarta Dictionary* as "the gradual acceptance by a person or group of the standards and practices of another person or culture."

enmeshment: refers to the "gooey" issues that bind the family together, indicative of a lack of boundaries and individuation within a dysfunctional family. Individuals are not free to make their own choices, come and go with freedom, and must stay bound together in their sickness.

family of origin: the family in which one was raised; mother and father, siblings, grandparents, aunts, uncles, foster care, and so on.

family of origin roles: parents assign roles consciously or unconsciously to children. Children act out these roles. These roles are: assigned patient, hero child, little parent, lost child, mascot, mediator, offender, perfect child, scapegoat, victim, perfect child, enabler, little princess, and little mother. Sharon Wegscheider-Cruse addresses some of these roles in her book, *Choicemaking* (Health Communications, Inc., 1985).

family of origin setup: the dysfunctional and/or addictive behaviors parents use to imprint a behavior on children.

family of origin work: the emotional and/or psychological work we do in therapy or with our sponsor in recovery that focuses on the ways we were set up in our original family of origin. It includes the grief work around those losses and areas of abuse and neglect.

family ordinals: the birth order of the children in the family.

fantasy and romance bonding: occurs when a relationship is built on the intellectual fantasizing and romanticizing in someone's head rather than the actual events and behaviors that occur within the relationship.

fantasy thinking: when we fantasize about how we want the relationship to be or we believe it to be a good relationship, rather than be in reality about the dysfunction, lack of honesty, and trusting our gut and intuition that something is wrong. Fantasy thinking is used as a way to "mood alter" from the pain we are feeling in our body, mind, and spirit, as well as a means to avoid dealing with our own pain about a relationship.

fix: when a co-sex addict tries to stop offensive behavior of a sex addict by giving more sex, being more seductive, more beautiful, and/or more forgiving.

grief work: as a result of growing up in a dysfunctional/addictive and/or neglectful family of origin, there are losses we experience on an emotional, spiritual, physical, and intellectual level. These losses must be acknowledged and grieved in recovery in order to have authentic relationships in present time.

guilt: the internal feeling we experience when we have done an offensive behavior that contradicts our own value system. When we experience guilt, it calls our attention to our own behaviors and the possibility that amends are in order.

healing work: action taken to cleanse one of offensive behavior or to get out of the victim role.

hero child: a term that originated from the work of Virginia Satir and Sharon Wegscheider-Cruse. It refers to the child in the family, often the oldest, who is the "superkid," high achiever, caretaker, and the one who attempts to bring positive attention and regard to the family.

inappropriate bond: when a person of power, such as an adult with a child, uses that power to bond in an unhealthy way with the child. Examples include a child taking care of a parent, an adult using a child sexually, or an authority figure of any sort using power to connect emotionally or sexually with another human being for their sole gratification.

incest: family members having sex with other members of their family.

incest survivor: one who accepts their reality and deals with the feelings about their family sexual abuse.

innate emotions: the instinctual feelings within us.

innate sense: the place inside ourselves where our intuitive "knowing" lives. In our culture, this sense is not nurtured, encouraged, or developed, and in an abusive/addictive environment, it is rejected. In an abusive/addictive dynamic, this innate sense must be eliminated in order for the offender/abuser to have consistent control over his victim.

intellectual abuse: occurs in a family environment and/or relationships in which members of the family or relationship are discouraged from thinking and questioning in general. There is an unspoken message that says "don't think" and/or "don't question," and especially "don't challenge" what is going on in the family and/or the relationship. The offender(s) creates an environment of secrecy and "crazy making" so that the victim(s) in the situation remains under his influence.

intervention: when members of the family or relationship begin to see the disease and addictive dynamic for what it is and take action to interrupt these addictive behaviors within the system. Trained, professional interventionists often assist in the interruptions of the addictive dynamic and are able to point people down the path of recovery and a new way of living. These paths may include family/individual therapy, 12-step recovery, treatment centers, and so on.

intimacy: sharing all of who we are, nonsexual, sexual, and sharing our feelings.

lack mentality: a term that has been developed to identify a way of thinking and behaving that we find pervades co-sex addiction and addictive dynamics. It refers to a core belief that "there is not enough." This belief may be conscious or unconscious and originates in our family of origin, in which there was a lack of physical, financial, emotional, and/or spiritual care. As adults we continue to hold this emptiness deep within and act it out with overeating, overspending, tolerating abuse in relationships, people pleasing, and so on as a continuation of trying to fill the emptiness and lack within.

little mother: a person who takes over the mothering role of her siblings in lieu of her mother.

little offender: see Big Victim and little offender

little parent: the child who takes on fathering or mothering his siblings.

little princess: the child who is designated as the "chosen one" by the father.

little victim: see Big Offender and little victim

lost child: one who is unseen by the family and carries the role everywhere.

mascot: this role is acted out to keep the family happy and keeps the focus off the abuse by being a clown.

mediator: this child tries to settle the differences between mother and father, and sometimes between other family members.

mirroring: behaviors that reflect another's actions.

obsession: the preoccupation with someone or something. For the sex addict, it is the preoccupation with a sexual "fix." For the co-sex addict, it is the preoccupation with the sex addict and/or the relationship.

offender: a person who perpetrates sexual, emotional, financial, spiritual, etc., abuse against a victim.

payoff: refers to what the co-sex addict receives, usually not conscious, by staying active in the addictive dynamic. For example, a co-sex addict may not confront behavior so that she does not have to experience her own fear of abandonment. Her payoff is avoiding this pain.

physical abuse: occurs whenever one uses physical, hurtful touch or threatens with physical touch to discipline, threaten, or otherwise control or manipulate someone else in a position of less power.

powerful serenity: the peace that comes from honest self-knowledge, particularly concerning our family of origin histories. It also comes from the empowerment of full self-expression, including having all of our feelings and using those feelings as tools to guide us in honoring our values, taking care of ourselves, and following our passions.

rage: a combination of shame and anger that has gone out of control. We believe in healthy anger. However, when anger is intensified and unexpressed over a period of time and combined with a shame reaction, rage will occur.

reality switch: when an active addict will manipulate reality in such a way that the other individual denies what she sees, feels, hears, and knows to be true in order to agree with and take on the addict's belief/reality. Thus, a switching of reality occurs.

recovery: the progressive restoration of spirit, mind, body, and emotional self from any form of addiction and/or any form of abuse or trauma. In the context of a 12-step program, we generally refer to this restoration as "recovery." Again, this speaks to the returning of spiritual, physical, emotional, and intellectual health.

religious addiction: the giving over of oneself and authentic spirituality to the rigid adherence to and obsession with rules and religious doctrines. Being addicted to religion is often an attempt to control, manipulate, and/or suppress feelings and behaviors of ourselves and others.

scapegoat: the individual in a dysfunctional system/relationship whose role is to take the focus off of the real, painful dynamics and addictive patterns in the family and/or relationship. This is often done by being blamed, dumped on, and punished in a group or relationship situation as a way to avoid individual responsibility for the addictive dynamics.

setup: a condition imposed upon the victim by anyone of power. Example: The setup for my co-sex addiction was by my parents.

set up: One is set up as a co-sex addict when she or he is sexually abused, covertly or overtly.

sex addiction: the act of giving up oneself for sex or sexual acting-out behaviors.

sexual abuse: occurs when one uses another sexually.

sexual anorexia: the lack of desire for sexual expression and/or sexual activities.

shame: the feeling that we are "not enough," are a "mistake," unworthy, undeserving, and generally "bad." We also believe that a God-given amount of shame can be described in a metaphor that sees the light touch of a butterfly as the amount of shame needed to let us know we are not God and to remember to put clothes on when we go out in public. We think that the shame one feels is often *carried shame*, which means that the victim of another's abuse carries the shame for this behavior while the offender is unable to experience his own healthy and appropriate remorse for his hurting/abusing of another person. When this occurs, we also refer to it as *shame dumping*.

shame dumping: see shame.

shame reduction: a therapeutic action taken to be rid of one's shame.

shut down: a term used when one is in her disease to such a degree that she is unable to connect with and verbalize her feelings, whether angry, sad, afraid, joyful, or shameful. When one is abused or lives in an addicted dysfunctional family system, it is often safer to close down feelings and separate ourselves from our feeling states, as this keeps us from feeling the painful emotions and loneliness that are present in this system.

silent rage: a behavior characterized by stuffing our anger and shame over time. This is an unspoken rage in which someone grows deeply silent with raging energy, and while no words are being spoken, this rage is palpable in its energy and quiet, powerful tension.

sponsorship: in 12-step programs, this refers to the choosing of an individual who has more time and experience in the program who can be our guide in formally working the 12 steps and integrating the tools of the program into our lives. We typically choose a sponsor by noticing our own attraction to another's recovery and/or recovery program and asking them if they are willing to sponsor us.

step work: written work centered on the 12 steps of co-sex addicts that Co-Sex Addicts Anonymous complete. Part of the work is to feel the feelings around those steps. This is shared with a sponsor.

stuffing feelings: a behavior we use that keeps our feelings repressed and hidden inside our bodies. This is a survival behavior when there is trauma, overwhelming feelings, and a lack of tools for healthy grieving and expressing emotions. There are several ways to stuff feelings. The primary way includes the use of drugs, alcohol, food, shopping, various forms of obsessive-compulsive behaviors, and/or sex addiction and co-sex addiction.

surrogate spouse: an individual, most often a child, who is substituted for the emotional and physical attention appropriately reserved for a spouse or partner in a marriage. Often a mother will look to her son for this support when the husband is emotionally or physically absent due to addiction. A parent may also use a daughter/son to be a "friend" who hears the complaints and frustrations with their partner and/or marriage.

survivor: when one survives sexual, physical, emotional, financial, or spiritual abuse of any kind.

total disconnection: having no connection physically, emotionally, or mentally.

triangulation: a dysfunctional, learned behavior in which individuals will not speak directly to each other about issues that occur within their relationship. A triangle is created when one person in the relationship involves a third person by discussing the relationship with them. This creates someone consistently being in the middle of two other people's relationship with each other and interferes with direct and honest communication.

triggered: refers to when a situation in our present-day relationship(s) jolts us into an old pattern, feeling, belief, or memory from our past, and an old wound is reopened. It is an important behavior to notice within ourselves so we are able to continue to separate our histories from our present-day lives. It is a reminder of family of origin work that still needs healing, as well as teaching us how to take care of ourselves in our current relationships.

victim: the recipient of abuse.

Recommended Reading

Alcoholics Anonymous. 4th rev. ed. New York: Alcoholics Anonymous World Service, 2001.

Beattie, Melody. *The Language of Letting Go*. Center City, MN: Hazelden, 1990.

Bradshaw, John. *Creating Love: The Next Stage of Growth*. New York: Bantam Books, 1992.

————. *The Family*. Revised and expanded. Deerfield Beach, FL: Health Communications, Inc., 1990.

————. *Family Secrets: What You Don't Know Can Hurt You*. New York: Bantam Books, 1995.

————. *Homecoming: Reclaiming and Championing Your Inner Child*. New York: Bantam Books, 1990.

Carnes, Patrick, Ph.D. *A Gentle Path Through the Twelve Steps*. Hazelden Publishing & Educational Services, 1989.

————. *Out of the Shadows*. Center City, MN: First published by CompCare Publishers and Hazelden Publishing, 1994.

Kasl, Charlotte. *Women, Sex and Addiction*. New York: Harper & Row, 1989.

May, Gerald, MD. *Addiction and Grace*. New York: HarperCollins, 1988.

Moore, Thomas. *The Soul of Sex*. New York: HarperCollins, 1998.

Peck, M. Scott, MD. *The Road Less Traveled*. New York: Simon and Schuster, 1978.

Satir, Virginia. *Conjoint Family Therapy*. 3rd ed. rev. and expanded. Palo Alto, CA: Science and Behavior, 1983.

Sears, R. Robert, *American Sociological Review*, Vol. 15, No. 3 (June 1950), pp. 397–401, doi:10.2307/2087182, licensed to JSTOR by American Sociological Association.

Wegscheider-Cruse, Sharon. *Choicemaking*. Deerfield Beach, FL: Health Communications, Inc., 1985.

Williamson, Marianne. *A Woman's Worth*. New York: Random House, 1993.

Acknowledgments

First and foremost, I would like to thank my Higher Power and Spiritual Guides who have blessed me through this recovery journey of twenty years. Also, I wish to thank the recovering women who have been my sponsors, those I have sponsored, and sisters who have shared their stories and have been a place of sacred listening and loving for me to share mine. Most especially, I wish to acknowledge Claudine, whose life has been an example of living recovery and whose heart has loved me through the ups and downs of my own journey.

Many men have been my teachers in mirroring to me my many recovery lessons in authentic relationships. It has been a journey of trial and error, and my husband, Alan, has been worth all the trial and errors along the way. I thank him for his constant support of my "queen beeness" and his desire for me to live fully in my power and authenticity in every area of my life. I would also like to thank our children, Ben, Daniel, and Hannah, whose wisdom, generosity, and individuality are wonderful examples of the power of parents living in recovery.

—*Sally Bartolameolli*

J would like to thank the multitude of recovering women who helped make this book possible. I would like to give special thanks to my coauthor, Sally, whose wisdom and strength were a driving force for this book. When things became too heavy, her humor helped me get to the next page. I'd also like to thank Sally's husband, Alan, for all of his work on the charts, even though he was in Africa.

Many thanks go to each of my eight adult children, who were very supportive of my writing this book. Thanks to my son Tony for reading this work and for his praise. And for being the first to recognize and encourage our family to step into reality. Thanks to my daughter Nettie for doing her own family work and for being an example of a strong woman. I respect your knowledge of recovery. Thanks to my daughter Sissy for being the first to read this book, and to my son Tim for giving me legal advice pertaining to this book. Also, for all the hugs and smiles you give me every day. To my daughter Lisa for her undying support for the truth throughout the years of recovery. Thanks to my son Peter for being the first to tell me we had a "bestseller." To my son Phil whose endless attention helped us in the final months of writing and editing. Particularly, thanks for the hours of computer work you did throughout this book. Also, thanks to my granddaughter Chelsea for the beautiful charts she made for this book. Thanks to my son Matt for his legal advice about the business part of this book during my writing journey. To all my grandchildren and great grandchildren who provide *Tutu* (Hawaiian for grandmother) joy. Your brightness and love gave me the courage to write about my dark side as well as the joy of my recovery. My wish for my family is to realize and enjoy the imprint that recovery has left on this family.

Aloha to Nancy, my "sista," for all the support and editing. *Mahalo* for suggesting we go to Hawaii for a break during the writing of this book.

Thanks to my friend, surrogate brother, and mentor John Bradshaw, who shared in endless ways his love and knowledge for this book. Most of all, thanks to my husband, George, whose authentic love, recovery, and support kept me on this path. Our authentic relationship imprints our family tree. Also, to my Higher Power, who has been with me all along the way.

—*Claudine Pletcher*

Further, we both give our appreciation and acknowledgment to the following organizations and individuals who have inspired so many of us in our recovery and spiritual journey and in the writing of this book.

We wish to especially acknowledge all the pioneers in early family systems and addiction recovery in all arenas, including alcoholism, drug addiction, love and sex addiction, codependency, adult children of alcoholics, dysfunctional families, dieting and food addictions, and so on.

While we cannot possibly name you all, we thank you for your contributions and the gifts of sobriety and recovery for which you have assisted so many of us: the Center for Recovery Families; The Council on Alcohol and Drugs Houston; The Meadows and the great counselors, Janice, Fred, and John; Melody Beattie, Claudia Black, Carol Brown, Ann Clark, Sharon Cruse, Terry Kellogg, Rochelle Lerner, Dr. Gerald May, Alice Miller, Jerrold Mundis, Anne Wilson Schaef, Marianne Williamson, and most especially John Bradshaw.

Index

Page numbers followed by an *f* indicate figures.

About the Authors

Sally Bartolameolli has a master's degree in education and has spent years teaching emotionally and learning challenged children. She is a certified Shadow Work® facilitator and health counselor trained at the Institute of Integrative Nutrition and Columbia University. She is also a member of the American Association of Drugless Practitioners. She is a certified teacher and trainer of Quest/Lion's Club Social Skills and Drug Prevention Curriculum for parents and children.

Her eating disorder originally led her to her 12-step recovery journey. She is a recovering bulimic as well as a member of other 12-step communities. Her twenty years of working her own personal recovery program, in addition to her other training and professional work, give her a firsthand understanding of the devastation of the co-sex addiction disease and the gifts of recovery.

As a gifted and intuitive facilitator and teacher, Sally has led and taught seminars, weekend retreats, and workshops all over the country, focused on the healing empowerment of women. She has a special interest in creating safe and empowering communities that give voice to diversity and bring into balance strong feminine perspective and expression.

Sally is committed to assisting women in uncovering and healing their

addictive behaviors and the setup in our society and family systems. Once
addiction is addressed, it is Sally's belief that we are freed to explore and
connect with our deeper Soul purpose and unique way of sharing our gifts and
being of service in the world. She shares her time between her home in
Lagos, Nigeria, and Houston, Texas.

Claudine Pletcher's journey began twenty-five years ago when she hit
her own personal bottom in her disease and dysfunction. Claudine sought
assistance in uncovering her own trauma and set up for dysfunction and
learned from the early pioneers in family systems work. She is one of the
original women who brought the Co-Sex Addicts Anonymous program to
the Southwestern United States. She is also the founding member of a
women's retreat that has continued for more than twenty years and remains
a supporter of Co-Sex Addicts Anonymous and all other 12-step programs.

Her own amazing journey into recovery has been a guiding inspiration to
many. One of the driving forces behind the commitment to her own recovery journey has been making a difference in her family of forty-one and the
mentoring of other recovering women. Her study of family systems and
trauma resolution in her own life brought joy and intimacy beyond her
expectations, most especially in the transformation of her marriage from
dysfunction to one of recovery and authentic love. With this personal healing, she developed a profound love for co-sex addiction recovery and the difference it makes in the lives of women, their families, and their relationships.

Considering that all work and no play makes for dullness, Claudine has
been a figure on the national scene in the horse world. She has owned cham-
pions in the hunter and jumper arenas. These equine friends have allowed
her inner child to come and play.

Code #6683 • $14.95

Reaching and sustaining a state of
mindfulness is what makes or breaks successful recovery.

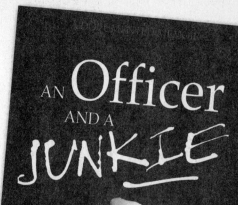